Playground Poets
Let your creativity flow...

South Wales
Edited by Steve Twelvetree

Young Writers

First published in Great Britain in 2005 by:
Young Writers
Remus House
Coltsfoot Drive
Peterborough
PE2 9JX
Telephone: 01733 890066
Website: www.youngwriters.co.uk

All Rights Reserved

© Copyright Contributors 2005

SB ISBN 1 84602 163 4

Foreword

Young Writers was established in 1991 and has been passionately devoted to the promotion of reading and writing in children and young adults ever since. The quest continues today. Young Writers remains as committed to the fostering of burgeoning poetic and literary talent as ever.

This year's Young Writers competition has proven as vibrant and dynamic as ever and we are delighted to present a showcase of the best poetry from across the UK. Each poem has been carefully selected from a wealth of *Playground Poets* entries before ultimately being published in this, our thirteenth primary school poetry series.

Once again, we have been supremely impressed by the overall high quality of the entries we have received. The imagination, energy and creativity which has gone into each young writer's entry made choosing the best poems a challenging and often difficult but ultimately hugely rewarding task - the general high standard of the work submitted amply vindicating this opportunity to bring their poetry to a larger appreciative audience.

We sincerely hope you are pleased with our final selection and that you will enjoy *Playground Poets South Wales* for many years to come.

Contents

Casllwchwr Primary School
Kimberley Davies (11)	1
Andrew Davies (10)	1
Scott Howells (11)	2
Sophie Williams (10)	2
Naomi Kitchin (10)	3
Catherine Taylor (11)	3
Jack Smith (11)	4
Alex Heaton (11)	4
Eluned Jones (10)	5
Lily Reece (10)	6
Emily Davies (10)	6
Jessica Blades-Sula (10)	6

Crumlin High Level Primary School
Zoe Walker (9)	7
Megan Hayward (9)	7
Harry Brown (8)	7
Donna Piacentini Davies (9)	7
Jessica Lillian May Box (9)	8
Kieran Phillips (9)	8
Lloyd Jones (9)	8
Charly Parker (8)	8
Kallum Williams (8)	9
Laura Kinson (9)	9
Emily Brown (8)	9
Francesca Hyde (9)	9
Sara Blanche (9)	10
Lydia Sweeney (11)	10
Emily Perry (10)	11
Garrod Fry (10)	11
Jamie Connett (9)	12
Rhys Davies (11)	12
William Davies (11)	13
Jonathan Llewellyn (11)	13
Jamie Baker (10)	14
Sophie Ashford (10)	14
Rosie Jones (10)	15
Liam Tetley (11)	15

Callum Jones (10)	16
Rebecca Nicklin (11)	16
Maddison Hazell (11)	17
Salman Ali (11)	17
Taylor Coles (10)	18
Damian Winnett (11)	18
Luke Davies (9)	19
Sophie Norman (9)	19
Jessica Davies (10)	20
Rhiannon Evans (11)	20
Samuel Brown (11)	21
Joel Valcic (10)	21
Jenna Hurn (9)	22
Rebecca Docherty (9)	22
Dion Tucker (9)	23
Elliot Gait (9)	23
Leah-Kate Howells (10)	24
Chloe Holtham (10)	24
Matthew Bourne (9)	25
Holly Gordon (9)	25
Megan Norris (9)	26
Kelly-Anne Edwards (11)	26
Ryan Bourne (9)	27
Emily Evans (11)	27
Fern Johnson (11)	28
Mercedes Parry (10)	28
Alex Gingell (10)	29
Jake Farmer (11)	29
Ryan Sayce (10)	30
Courtney Jones (10)	30
Emily Thomas (11)	31
Alex Toms (10)	31
Emily Leader (10)	32
Domonic Norman (7)	32
Alyssia Ward (9)	33
Calwyn Fry (7)	33
Brandon Hiscox (10)	34
Lewys James (7)	34
Liam Edwards (7)	34
Jed Hamar-Davies (7)	35
Craig Fletcher (8)	35
James Chivers (7)	35

Durham Road Junior School

Dylan John (9)	36
Jordan Pickering (8)	36
Corey Cosslett (9)	37
Amber Bendall (7)	37
Bethan Hill-Howells (9)	38
Olivia Bell (7)	38
Shorna Devney (9)	39
Lauren Russell (8)	39
Curtis Ayling (9)	40
Abigail Lewis (8)	40
Eleanor Mumford (7)	41
Caitlin Mazey (7)	41
Katie Gregory (8)	42
Mia Frost (8)	42
Morgan Roberts (7)	43
Benjamin Norvill (7)	43
Katie Dorling (8)	44
Jack Reese (7)	45
Freddie Mears (10)	45
Brogan Jones (8)	46
Isabel Reeves (7)	46
Hannah Cox (7)	47
William Davis (10)	47
Luke Orphan (8)	48
Sam Williams & Luke McCarthy (9)	48
Hannah Payne (7)	49
Matthew Collins (11)	49
Mark Delaney & Ben Reese (9)	50
Katie Upton (10)	50
Shannen Arnold (11)	51
Cheyenne Jayne-Manning (10)	51
Alex Collins (11)	52
Ben Reese (9)	52
Demi Micallef (10) & Ayeshah Behit (11)	53
Philip Dixon (10)	53
Luke Rogers (10)	54
Sam Orphan (9)	54
Dominic Little (10)	55
Jessie Harrhy (10)	55
Kristy Griffiths (11)	56
Sophie Challenger (8)	56

Name	Score
Joshua Burrows (10)	57
Bethan Jones (10)	57
Jack Lapthorn (10)	58
Jordan Kemp (10)	58
James Ford (10)	59
Samantha Reeves (10)	59
Jessica Haggerty (11)	60
Morgan Hoskins (8)	60
Jennifer Murphy (11)	61
Hope Merrick (8)	61
Emily Langford (10)	62
Timothy Berrow (10)	62
Megan Davies (8)	63
Rory Mitchell (9)	63
Danielle Sharpe (9)	64
Isobel Bayley (8)	64
Jessica Griffiths (8)	64
Jusef Behit (9)	65
Dorian Payne (9)	65
Isabel Broadribb (8)	65
Joseph Brown (8)	66
Olivia Gregory (9)	66
Bethan Porter (9)	67
Tinotenda Nyamunda (9)	67
Jarrod Lewis (9)	68
Amber Howell (8)	68
Jack Masters (9)	68
Johnny Sheeran (8)	69
Ellie Hopkins (8)	69
Oliver Dowie (8)	69
Harvey Abraham-Evans (8)	70
Jake Abraham (8)	70
Stephanie England (9)	70
Ben Heath (9)	71
Rebecca Farley (9)	71
Rebecca Taylor (8)	72
Andrew Sprudd (8)	72
Joe Palmer-Phillips (8)	73
Bradley Bushell (8)	73

Gaer Junior School
Hannah Victoria Snelling (10)	74
Alexandra Blackley (10)	74
Matthew Thorn	74
Jamie Reed (11)	75
Lauren Hillier (10)	76
Annalize James (11)	76
Matthew Perrin (11)	76
Fedor Tot (11)	77
Rhys John Harries (9)	77
Anna Corten (10)	77
Katie Heard (10)	78
Cherie Crighton (8)	78
Mark Goddard (11)	79
James Morgan (11)	79
Amy Turner (10)	80
Dean McDonald (9)	80
Luke Johnson (9)	81
Ben Ford Weaver (8)	81
Thomas Sayce-Upton (10)	81
Curtis Macias (10)	82
Abigail Emily Coe (9)	82
Jack Evans (9)	83
Joshua Dominic Bertie (9)	83
Kyle McCarthy (8)	84
Adrienne Bartlett (9)	84
Hannah Louise Morgan (9)	84
James Luckett (8)	85

Gorseinon Junior School
Emily O'Dwyer & Ryan Lewis (10)	85
Jack Seaward (7)	86
Steven Jones (7)	86
David Davies & Jordan Yemm (10)	87
Ben Davies (7)	87
Class Y6D (10)	88
Dafydd Thomas (7)	89

Llangiwg Primary School
Rowan Joseph-Lake	89
Zoe Jagoe-Williams	89

Annie Hughes (10) — 90
Kate Thomas — 90
Nathan Blackler — 90

Millbrook Junior School
Valmai Dearden (8) — 91
Anthony Lloyd (11) — 91
Katie Colborne (11) — 92
Alura Devlin (7) — 92
Luke Morgan (10) — 93
Alexander William Leighton (11) — 93
Curtis Shiers (9) — 94
Amy Davies (9) — 95
Ben Simms (10) — 96
Samantha Jo Elliott (11) — 97
Ashley Bastow (11) — 97
Alana Dalton-Francis (7) — 98
Bradley Satchell (10) — 98
Chelsie Cadman (11) — 99
Joanne Morgan (10) — 99
Kai Jones (11) — 100
Joshua Skillern (10) — 100
Conor Gough (11) — 100
Brogan Keepin (11) — 101
Sarah Archer (10) — 101
Gemma Bates (10) — 101
Rhys Coulson (11) — 102
Emily Ann Merry (11) — 102
Jordanne Leigh Setterfield (8) — 103
Holly Goldsworthy (11) — 103
Ben Fisher (11) — 103
Joshua Edwards (11) — 104
Ryan Smith (11) — 104
Rebecca Jade Duke (10) — 105
Billie Lee Palmer (10) — 105
Jacob Richards (9) — 106
Morgan Lingard & Kyle Vodden (10) — 106
Kristoffer Maybry (9) — 107
Alicia Redman (10) — 108
Louis Hillberg & Jack Watkins (10) — 109
Chloe Smith (9) — 110

Alice Kate Pritchard (10)   111
Michael Moynihan (10)   111

Penyrheol Primary School
Morgan Elliott (8)   112
Ellie Evans (7)   112
Amy Gibbons (8)   113
Nicholas Powell (8)   113
Emelia Russell (9)   114
Zoe Belton (8)   114
Victoria Robinson (7)   115
Sophie Davies (8)   115
Courtney Evans (9)   116
Curtis Hovvels (7)   116
Sam Woods (9)   117
Anya Russell (8)   117
Zak Fisher (8)   118
Gethin Sullivan (7)   118
Alexander Murphy (7)   119
Lee Jones (8)   119
Liam Matthews (9)   120
Samuel Matthews (8)   120

St Joseph's Cathedral Juniors, Swansea
Ellie Donohoe (7)   121
Ellie May Diamond (7)   121
Jordan Baker (8)   121
Ryan Argyle (9)   122
Emily Draper (8)   123
Joshua Nedin (8)   124
Ryan Dark (8)   124
Lauren Ward (8)   125
Sougri Abugre (8)   125
Robin Bermudez (9)   126
Emily Cooney (8)   126
Kirra Williams (8)   126
Sophie Lloyd (8)   127
Atlanta Martone (8)   127
Georgia Davies (7)   127
Alicia McCabe (9)   128
Katie Davis (7)   128

Lucy Jenkins (8)	128
Luke Cardone (8)	129
Joel Wayne Morris (8)	129
Callum Daniel (9)	129
Rhys Jones (8)	130
Lauren Baskerville (8)	130
Chloe Hayden (9)	131
John Collins (9)	131
Joseph Thomas (9)	132
Ben Lloyd (9)	132
Anthony Loibl (9)	132
Sarah Passmore (8)	133
Scott Hopkins (8)	133
Jordan Bevan (8)	134
Connah Troy (8)	134
Chelsea Jones (7)	134
Sean McCabe (9)	135
Keeanna Cullen (7)	135
Leah Palmer (7)	135
Lily Thomas (7)	136
Samuel Reseigh (7)	136
Dylan Driscoll (8) & Lorna Cozens (7)	137
John Bermudez (8)	137
Caitlin Dorrell-Hunt (7)	138
Kieran Parkhouse (8)	138
Jessica Davies (8)	139
Jade Barry (7)	139
Nicole O'Connell (8)	139
Sophie Morgan-Key (8)	140
Jake Hoskin (8)	140
Daniel Duggins (7)	140
Anthony Barletta (8)	141

St Monica's CW Primary School, Cardiff

Dyfri Schmidhamer (11)	141
Michele Montersino (8)	142
Rimsha Ali (9)	142
Gbenga Omirinde (10)	143
Sulli Richards (9)	143
Joe Jones (8)	144
Ben Jones (10)	144

Danielle Nicole Paglionico (9)	145
Jacob Fenner (9)	145
Sophie Lauren Bowen (10)	146
David Lee Flynn (10)	146
Bethan Anne Watts (10)	147
Alice Wellock (8)	147
David Rogers (10)	148
Megan Davies (10)	148
Pearl Mlambo (11)	149
Mohamed Binesmael (11)	150
Tor Richards (11)	150
Fairooz Mostafa (10)	150

St Peter's RC Primary School, Cardiff

Shorna Marie Buckley (9)	151
Huw Thompson (10)	151
Lauren Anne Byrne (9)	152
Ryan Spriggs (10)	153
Taylor Nicholson (10)	154
Jessica Caitlin Sidney (9)	155
Shane Geoghegan (9)	156
Ellen Lewis (9)	157
Joseph Elford (10)	158
Milo Cashin (8)	158
Samantha Downey (9)	159
Siobhan Quigley (9)	159
Lauren Copeland (10)	160
Toby Andrews (10)	161
Giorgia Racis (9)	162
Dhana Davis (10)	163
Mary Shaw (10)	164
Jake Andrews (10)	164
Kaitlin Patterson (8)	165
Ben Elias (7)	165
Jack Lynham (8)	166
Rachel Edwards (9)	166
Sophie Manley (9)	167
Conor Meehan (8)	168
Ben Parker (8)	169
Joseph Clarke (8)	170
Jake Vella (9)	171

Kieran Nolan (8)	172
Christian Nunan (9)	173
Connor Greet (9)	174
Philippa O'Sullivan (10)	175
Christy Ring (10)	176
Sneha Babu (9)	177
Dominique Davies (9)	178
Rachel Morgan (10)	179
Philip Campigli (10)	180
Connor Price (10)	181
Madi Parle-Smith (7)	182
Chelsea Beaumont (8)	183
Ryan Donovan (9)	184
Eleanor Davis (9)	185
Jonathan Dart (10)	186
Adrian Williams (9)	187
Lauren Leslie (9)	188
Kate Ryan (10)	189

Thornwell Primary School

Megan Thomas (8)	189
Daniel Wroe (11)	190
Jacob Graham-Dobrowolny (8)	190
Brittany Oliver (7)	190
Kelsey Gittoes (11)	191
Ashleigh Ann Fawcett (9)	191
Rachael Sims (10)	191
Stacey Gittoes (11)	192
Lucy James (11)	192
Skye Taylor (11)	192
Charlene Williams (10)	193
Luke Payne (10)	193
Cade Beacham (10)	193
Amy Huyton (11)	194
Ryan Harley-Powell (11)	194
Ryan Palmer (10)	194
Marcus Arrowsmith (10)	195
Alex Methuen (8)	195
Robyn Evans (10)	195
Jennifer Thomas (7)	196
Yiesha Weir (8)	196

Sophie Gresswell (8)	196
Daniel Tyler (9)	197
Harriet Ling (10)	197
Jonathan Davies-Whyatt (9)	198
Mason Segal (11)	198
Edward Neal (10)	198
Abigail Watts (11)	199
Jordan Gough (10)	199
Tracey Roberts (11)	200
Kirsten Jones (11)	200
William Tregaskes (10)	201
Ellie Neye-Williams (10)	201
James Edinborough (10)	201
Sophie Bennett (10)	202
Kieran Brewer (10)	202
Lydia Ferriman (10)	202
Emma Giles (11)	203
Siobhan Rogers (10)	203
Ryan Thomas (11)	204
Jack Pearce-Webb (11)	204
Chloe Drake (11)	205
Kristie Harry (10)	205
Alex Pelling (10)	206
Nikaela Methuen (10)	206
Lee Haines (11)	207
Michael Lowe (10)	207
Charlotte Davies (11)	208
Kyle Harry (10)	209
Shay Hill (9)	209
Chloe Adams (8)	210
Matthew Barnes (11)	210
Amie Morgan (9)	211
Joel Butcher (9)	211
Georgia Brown (8)	212
Shannon Smith (8)	212
Sam Greening (9)	212
Holly Poole (11)	213

Whitestone Primary School

Jasmin Davies (9)	213
Emily Stevens (10)	214

Kizzi Parry (9)	214
Amy Smith (9)	214
Saul Moore (10)	215
Josie Ransome (10)	215
Jessica Link (9)	215
Katie Williams (10)	216
Rhiannon Robinson (9)	217
Sam Davies (10)	217

The Poems

Through The Door Into The Mysterious Garden

Here I stand in front of the door waiting for my hand to
Slip and open it.

Behind the door I imagine a long lane of green emerald grass
With a greenhouse standing proudly,
As hyacinths blossom the air pushes their stems.

Under the door the air crawls and comes up
And brushes my hair.

The summerhouse is like the rest of the garden,
Asleep on its feet.

Beyond the pond and the summerhouse is another path
Meandering in idle curves.

As I go through the door I see a greenhouse as big as a giant's
House, taking me in.

I stand, imagining mountains and fields
And yew trees and birds singing.

As I close the door, I return to my bed
And I dream of the mysterious garden,
As it waits for me to come back.

Kimberley Davies (11)
Casllwchwr Primary School

Metaphor Poetry - My Mum

She is a silk, white, shining pillow waiting for me
To embrace her when I get home.
She is a beautiful, sleek, yellow cat rubbing up to me.
Her voice is a choir of angels.
She is the shining star in my night's eye.
She is the wonderful summer month of August.
She is a warm tasty apple pie baked in my heart.
If she is as big as the Millennium Stadium
Or if she is as small as a doll,
She will always be the biggest person for love in my heart.

Andrew Davies (10)
Casllwchwr Primary School

Africa

If Africa was a colour it would be the golden sunsets
Which fill the sky every night.

If Africa was a sound it would be the roaring of a lion
Ready to devour its prey, calling its family to feast.

If Africa was an animal it would be the fast lunging Nile
Crocodile snatching its prey from the river.

If Africa was a sport it would be a fast game of cricket
Being played in South Africa.

If Africa was a food it would be a freshly killed pig
Just about to be shared around the manyatta.

If Africa was a flower it would be a yellow rose
Like the savannah.

If Africa was a mood it would be lazy and relaxed
Under the sunset.

If Africa was a drink it would be blood which is sucked
Out of an animal by the Masai tribe.

If Africa was music it would be a slow steady beat of
Native African drums.

Scott Howells (11)
Casllwchwr Primary School

My Nan

She is a soft and cosy bed cover
In silky velvet, when I go and cuddle up
She brightens the room.
She is a nice furry rabbit who makes the sound of a puppy.
She brings the cold snow to my face that gives me
The twinkle of Christmas in December.
She is a nice crunchy chip and a soothing drink.
She is a shining bike that plays with me.
She is a big shop that spoils me.
When we go outside I can hear the rustle of her wheels.

Sophie Williams (10)
Casllwchwr Primary School

My Great Gran

She is a cosy, rich, velvet armchair that pulls me with my toes pointing.
She is a cute little robin with a shiny red rose breast who tweets
as the fiery sun appears upon the crystal glass mountain.
She is the tapping of cold white snow on my face, like angels
falling from Heaven.
She is the month of January, who brings the spring onto winter
to melt the snow.
She is the ripeness of fruit who refreshes your throat.
She is the glowing of a boat in the twilight rocking on the harbour sea,
that brightens the world.
She is the Tudor house with a hot burning fire that warms my body,
like the golden sun.
She is the time for bath with wrinkled hands and fingertips.
She is the colour of beige and the smell of a green grass grapevine.
She is the queen from an ancient world.

Naomi Kitchin (10)
Casllwchwr Primary School

My Grandmother

She is an antique possession sitting upon the shelf
Wrapped in a duvet of dust.

She is a waddling duck who's lost her quack and her
Feathers have turned all grey.

The purring of a cat floats in the room.

She is the sun beaming down on a hot summer's day.

Her spring happiness affects everyone else.

She is a golden crumpet drowned in butter and sugar
And sweet honey.

Her transport isn't a car anymore.

She is a building that is short and stumpy,
The colour if any is grey.

Catherine Taylor (11)
Casllwchwr Primary School

Africa

If Africa was a colour, it would be the hot golden sand of the Sahara Desert, as the sun blasts light onto the surface like a torch.

If Africa was a sound, it would be the loud roar of a lion
Defending its territory as the wild deer came.

If Africa was an animal, it would be a silver elephant
As it walks and breaks the trees,
Its long trunk grabs the brown tall tree like a child hugging his mum.

If Africa was a sport it would be the tribes throwing their javelins -
They soar through the air as fast as light and hit the bull which will be eaten tonight.

If Africa was a food it would be a red-hot chilli fresh from its plant,
As hot as the sun, it is a fireball that hits the tongue.

If Africa was a flower it would be a hard cactus standing like a soldier
As the heat and the little fresh breeze flaps through its stem.

If Africa was a mood it would be a relaxed one that went on forever,
Like a holiday in Spain, nothing to do but laze around.

If Africa was a drink it would be a bottle of red wine,
As red as blood and the colour of sunset and the bitter taste.

If Africa was music it would be the sound of a symbol
As the sun crashes onto the green layered forest.

Jack Smith (11)
Casllwchwr Primary School

My Brother

He is a new little wooden stool that's hard,
He is a lion ready to pounce,
A large foghorn always sounding,
He is the cold, wet showers of April,
He is the hot and spicy vindaloo curry,
He is a Ferrari speeding down the road,
He is a massive skyscraper towering above everything.

Alex Heaton (11)
Casllwchwr Primary School

The Garden Ghost

As my hand goes through the door,
I don't feel it anymore.

I push and pull to get it out
At this point now there is no doubt.

I'm finally through,
I'm feeling numb too.

My footprints aren't there, but who's are they?
A dark black figure comes my way.

A dark figure wearing a blood red, rusty dress.
It is all dark and ancient, it is in a mess.

In the window the whiteness of a face,
My heart is beating fast like the human race.

Who's there? What's happening?
It's starting to get a bit too frightening.

I smell the fear
As I get near.

In the darkness of the night
I see the yew trees not looking right.

Before I reach the bottom of the garden,
The moon has disappeared.

The trees are dancing wildly in the winter's storm,
In its weird, freaky form.

Demons of the air let loose around me,
They are all very free.

Silence, not a twig breaks,
Until a human cry awakes.

Fire hits a giant as it falls through the sky,
Little ashes and leaves set off to fly.

As I finally touch the door handle,
A hand falls on my back and . . .

Eluned Jones (10)
Casllwchwr Primary School

My Cousin

She is a comfortable new velvet settee.
She is a blade of grass dancing in the breeze.
She is a sleeping puppy breathing heavily.
She is summer.
June, July, August.
A lush juicy apple.
A beautiful sports car.
A beauty salon.

Lily Reece (10)
Casllwchwr Primary School

White To Me Is . . .

Cotton candy clouds
Floating over my head.
Peace and silence fading
Into the mist.
Pearly white gates
Leading into the sunset.
Pleasant ice cream on a sunny, afternoon.
Icy frost on a cold winter morning.

Emily Davies (10)
Casllwchwr Primary School

How I See Indigo

A penetrating glow of disguise.
The colour of a wizard's cloak luminous in darkness.
A forgotten passage of time.
A sunset that is continuous.
A mystery that is never solved.

Jessica Blades-Sula (10)
Casllwchwr Primary School

Willow Tree Haiku

Willow tree crying
With overhanging branches
Flooding the river.

Zoe Walker (9)
Crumlin High Level Primary School

The Willow Tree Haiku

Willow tree standing,
Tears falling down to the ground,
Without any sound.

Megan Hayward (9)
Crumlin High Level Primary School

Willow Tree Haiku

Willow tree stands with
Tears falling to the stream which
Sadly flows away.

Harry Brown (8)
Crumlin High Level Primary School

The Willow Tree Haiku

Willow tree hanging
With tears falling in the stream
Making the stream gleam.

Donna Piacentini Davies (9)
Crumlin High Level Primary School

The Apple Tree Haiku

Apple tree standing,
With apples under the tree,
Who will pick them up?

Jessica Lillian May Box (9)
Crumlin High Level Primary School

Doves Haiku

One dove passing by
Two doves with pretty white wings
Joined by one more dove.

Kieran Phillips (9)
Crumlin High Level Primary School

Doves Haiku

Two doves flying high
Soaring in the sky softly
Pushing the wind by.

Lloyd Jones (9)
Crumlin High Level Primary School

The River Haiku

A river flowing,
Quickly past the willow tree,
To the open sea.

Charly Parker (8)
Crumlin High Level Primary School

River Haiku

A river flowing,
Gently through the riverbed,
Leaves are falling down.

Kallum Williams (8)
Crumlin High Level Primary School

Willow Tree Haiku

Willow tree growing,
A willow tree standing high,
Willow tree blowing.

Laura Kinson (9)
Crumlin High Level Primary School

Doves Haiku

Pretty doves flying,
Representing lovely peace,
Flying high above.

Emily Brown (8)
Crumlin High Level Primary School

Willow Tree Haiku

Willow tree standing
Moving its leaves and branches
Leaves look like crying.

Francesca Hyde (9)
Crumlin High Level Primary School

Weather Haikus

Hail
Bounces off rooftops
And scatters across the floor
In its white, hard coat.

Fog
It comes from nowhere
It looks like a white blanket
It is hard to see.

Sun
It shines very bright
Like a big glowing fire ball
Yellowy and bright.

Thunder
It sounds like a drum
Makes young children very scared
Banging all day long.

Sara Blanche (9)
Crumlin High Level Primary School

Evacuee

I can see the trees going past,
Children crying for their families,
I can see other children having a blast,
And others sat silently.

I can feel sadness,
And the train going fast.
I can feel madness
And I hope the day doesn't last.

I can hear the train chugging,
And the wheels going round.
I can hear people bugging
And a funny sound.

Lydia Sweeney (11)
Crumlin High Level Primary School

Weather Haikus

Thunder
Banging and clanging
Giving people a big fright
Making the sky dark.

Sun
Shining through the clouds
Making our world beautiful
Making people hot

Lightning
Crashing to the floor
Electric bolts everywhere
Brightening the sky.

Hurricane
Going all around
Crashing peoples' belonging
Rebuilding their lives.

Emily Perry (10)
Crumlin High Level Primary School

Soldier

Dark skies, mums crying,
Children getting on the train,
They start to leave,
Upset without their mums.

Children breaking their hearts,
Mums crying a lot.
Parents sad, missing their children.
All in pain.

Rain starting to fall,
Children crying,
Puddles forming on the ground,
The train ready to go.

Garrod Fry (10)
Crumlin High Level Primary School

Weather Haikus

Hurricane
A crackling bashing
A raging forky cutter
And floor opens wide.

Lightning
A zigzagging fork
Like a big flying arrow
With great belting wings.

Sun
A ball of gases
A fiery blazing fire ball
The beam of the strike.

Snow
A cold, icy freeze
White furry coat shivering
Blowing and smashing.

Jamie Connett (9)
Crumlin High Level Primary School

Evacuee

I can see the big train.
The wheels running,
The steam above me,
And the parents crying.

I feel the excitement
And the nerves twitching,
My belly's rumbling,
I feel my dad has died.

I hear children screaming
And the steam engine
And the people sobbing,
And then I hear the teacher.

Rhys Davies (11)
Crumlin High Level Primary School

Soldier

Bombs being dropped
German planes flying across the sky
Guns shooting at the planes
And men screaming in pain.

Pain in my heart
Sadness for my children
Pain in my head
Blooding down my arm.

Loudness from the siren,
Noise from one hundred planes,
People screaming for help,
Me screaming in pain.

William Davies (11)
Crumlin High Level Primary School

Soldier

We all see a dark cloud approaching,
We all see death coming,
We all see people crying,
Guns firing to the war.

We see dads' feelings about children.
They want to protect their child.
They want to be brave.
They want to stop the war.

I can hear bombs dropping.
I can hear guns firing.
I can hear people asking for their lives.
I can hear planes coming for war.

Jonathan Llewellyn (11)
Crumlin High Level Primary School

Soldier

There's a dark cloud hanging over the sky.
People fighting for their lives because they don't want to die.
Planes are dropping bombs when they're flying
All the soldiers are scared and are running.

You can feel the blood coming out of the men
When you're killing a chicken or stabbing a ram.
You can feel all the men crawling and crying
Shouting, 'Help me, I've just got shot!'

You can hear the banging of the guns
When you couldn't even rest to eat some buns.
You can hear the soldiers crying for help
Because the blood is pouring from their heads.

Jamie Baker (10)
Crumlin High Level Primary School

Evacuee

I can see children crying for their mummies.
Looking through the windows flying past the trees,
I can see the station, I can see a shop.
I can see Wales now and we're coming to a stop.

I can feel sadness all around me,
I can feel vibration coming through the seats,
I can feel the train chugging along the line,
I can feel my teddy bear because he's mine, all mine.

I can hear loud screeches and screams,
I can hear children wanting ice cream.
I can hear my teacher checking through the list,
Let's hope that nobody is missed.

Sophie Ashford (10)
Crumlin High Level Primary School

Evacuee

A mother and child waving goodbye
Trying to hold it in but wanting to cry.
The train is on its way
I really don't want to go away.

Sadness is how I'm feeling from head to toe,
I really wish this sad pain would go.
Without my family it doesn't feel right,
I miss my mum and I cry all night.

The whistle blow of the train
The tip and tapper of the rain
The crying and the sadness of my friend
Hoping this World War would soon end.

Rosie Jones (10)
Crumlin High Level Primary School

Soldier

I can see people ignored, people killing,
People dying and people shooting.
Bombs dropping, people running and big explosions.
People homeless and children carrying suitcases.

I can feel the rain trickling on my hands
My heart pounding and pounding with fright.
The blood pouring down my leg from a sharp object,
I feel scared.

I can hear screams of people dying,
Children hurt and I hear them crying,
And a lieutenant shouting, 'Fire!'
I can hear big bangs from bombs being dropped
And the air raid siren going off.

Liam Tetley (11)
Crumlin High Level Primary School

Soldier

I can see bombs blowing up,
I can see tanks firing at their enemy,
I can see men shooting with guns,
I can see men running to stay alive.

I can feel mud on my feet,
I can feel rain dripping down my face,
I can feel my feet hurting while running,
I can feel my arm hurting from holding my gun.

I can hear gun fire,
I can hear bombs landing,
I can hear shouting from my friends,
I can hear shouting for help.

Callum Jones (10)
Crumlin High Level Primary School

Soldier

I can see bombs rushing through the sky,
Blood being stained into the ground,
Men running with their guns for their lives,
Dirty men shooting in the trenches.

I can feel my feet aching as I run,
My ears being deafened from the noise,
My head telling me what to do,
My eyes hurt from the mud going in them.

I can hear the screams from my friends,
The bombs going off with a bang,
The shouts of help from the other soldiers dying,
The shoots of guns aiming at me.

Rebecca Nicklin (11)
Crumlin High Level Primary School

Evacuee

I can see the smoke above me,
Children crying and sobbing next to me,
The trees and bushes flying past me,
The driver in the front seat driving me.

I can feel the plastic seats underneath me,
I feel coldness and sadness inside me,
The wetness of the window beside me,
My mum's warm clothes around me.

I can hear the train wheels beneath me,
Children sobbing uncontrollably,
I'm shaking nervously,
At last, we're in Wales!

Maddison Hazell (11)
Crumlin High Level Primary School

Evacuees

Children are waving on the train
Outside it's tippling down with rain.
Some are happy and some are sad,
Some are injured and some are bad.

Tears going through my eyes,
I was just about to cry.
Mum's crying, they're feeling the pain,
I'm so scared.

People crying for their mummies,
Everyone caring for their babies.
A child crying, someone punched him,
And his name is Tim.

Salman Ali (11)
Crumlin High Level Primary School

Weather Haikus

Lightning
Zigzag through the air
The blinding bolts of lightning
Bright lights fill the air.

Rain
Splash, splash on the roads
Water goes down the canals
Puddles all around.

Snow
On the floor cold snow
Wearing their fluffy white coats
Where it turns to ice.

Hail
Throp, throp on the ground
Sprinkle, sprinkle in the world
Move we're coming down.

Taylor Coles (10)
Crumlin High Level Primary School

Soldiers

Soldiers crying for their lives,
Bombs flying through the air,
Tanks and guns shooting everywhere,
Bangs and bombs.

The rain twinkling on your head,
Blood running down your head,
My heart beating as I hold a gun,
I am feeling scared.

Damian Winnett (11)
Crumlin High Level Primary School

Weather Haikus

Fog
Grey mist creeping by
Headlights going bright and white
Look it's dangerous.

Hail
Water hammering down
Ready to fall and explode
In its big thick coat.

Lightning
Zigzag lines shooting
The colour yellow falling
Hitting the ground hard.

Rain
All its pittering
Everything being soaked
Everybody sighs.

Luke Davies (9)
Crumlin High Level Primary School

Weather Haikus

Fog
Snow creeping darkness
Like an eerie mist in the
Spooky moonlit sky.

Snow
Slowly creeping down
Like a white tree in springtime
Flowing softly down.

Rain
Like a waterfall
It flows down a mountain spring
Into the ocean.

Sophie Norman (9)
Crumlin High Level Primary School

Dragon Land

Wouldn't you like to go to Dragon Land
Where you can lie out on the sand?
You'll gasp when you see the entrance
There it is so big and proud,
It makes you want to scream out loud.

The dragon's food in my hand,
Then it yells get off my land.
The food there is great, fried people,
Well the food is good to the dragons.

I hear the screams of children on the dragon rides
The children like it, you'll be surprised.
The dragons are stomping their feet like mad
Because in Dragon Land, it will always make you glad.

Jessica Davies (10)
Crumlin High Level Primary School

Evacuee

Dark clouds moving overhead,
Everybody sitting on their nice comfy beds.
People sobbing, cuddled up
Everybody saying, 'Come and pick me up!'

Feeling sad, feeling glum
They come and give you a chewing gum.
Feeling quite excited, never been on a train,
Feeling quite happy, going on a plane.

Crying, sobbing, muttering, sad.
Lots and lots of children feeling really bad.
Hearing the train cluttering away,
Hear them crying day after day!

Rhiannon Evans (11)
Crumlin High Level Primary School

World War

I see . . .
The bombs exploding, making an explosion,
The fire of the guns, people diving to the ground,
The army taking prisoners to POW camps,
The city getting burnt to the ground.

I feel . . .
The sparks of fire flying off the flames,
The gun strapped so tightly around my waist,
The mud in the trenches getting in my shoes,
The explosives in my pocket waiting to be thrown.

I hear . . .
The fire of the guns shooting people to the ground,
The soldiers shouting, 'Go on!' to each other,
The burning of the buildings crashing to the ground,
I can hear the gunshots fading,
I close my eyes and slowly fade away.

Samuel Brown (11)
Crumlin High Level Primary School

The Football Game

I can see the flying football
Smashing into the net
I can see the amazing big stadium
It's a really first class set.

I can feel the tension
When he steps up for the free kick,
I can feel the relief when he scores the goal.
The other team will be sick.

I can hear the clang of the post
When the ball goes just wide.
I can hear the roar of the crowd
We won! We won! Hard game you will find.

Joel Valcic (10)
Crumlin High Level Primary School

Weather Haikus

Sun
Everyone is out
On the beaches everywhere
Having loads of fun.

Rain
It's all coming down
Pitter-patter on the road
Then it all dries up.

Snow
The sky is cloudy
The road is covered in snow
It is really cold.

Lightning
It lights up the sky
The sky is brightly lit up
The fork is out, *crash!*

Jenna Hurn (9)
Crumlin High Level Primary School

Weather Haikus

Snow
Little snowflakes fall
Nearly every winter time
In the fluffy coats.

Rain
Rain, rain coming down
Pitter-patter goes the rain
Splish splash in puddles.

Sun
Sun, sun shine so bright
Bright up the world with your light
Everyone laughing.

Rebecca Docherty (9)
Crumlin High Level Primary School

Weather Haikus

Sun
Red-hot scorching beam
Shining brightly from the sky
Drying up rivers.

Lightning
Zigzag in the sky
Yellow lightning zooming down
Crashing on the road.

Thunder
Crashing in the clouds
It's making very loud noise
May be dangerous.

Rain
Precipitation
Comes down like a waterfall
Evaporation.

Dion Tucker (9)
Crumlin High Level Primary School

Weather Haikus

Sun
It's a red blazing
Ball of fire up in the sky
Ready to explode.

Rain
Splish splash rain falling
Puddles forming on the ground
Put caps and coats on.

Snow
The cold, thick, white snow
Covering the ground quickly
Let's make a snowman.

Elliot Gait (9)
Crumlin High Level Primary School

Weather Haikus

Snow
Children play in it
The soft snowflakes coming down
Ice skating is here.

Rain
Precipitation
Squishing, squelching in the mud
No going outside.

Lightning
Zigzags in the sky
Darting across so quickly
In the dark blackness.

Thunder
Bang, bang goes thunder
Crish, crash through the dark night sky
Scaring the children.

Leah-Kate Howells (10)
Crumlin High Level Primary School

Weather Haikus

Wind
Rustling through the trees
Blowing down the long bright streets
Colder and colder.

Rain
Precipitation
Dazzling on my two wet arms
Drip drop here it comes.

Sun
Playing out on grass
Going for picnics in heat
Gigantic fireball.

Chloe Holtham (10)
Crumlin High Level Primary School

Weather Haikus

Sun
A fast water slide,
Blazing sunshine all around
Scorching ball of fire.

Snow
It's a white blanket
Bang! A snowball hits me hard
Snowflakes fall gently.

Rain
The ground's very wet
It patters off the rooftops
It makes me feel sad.

Fog
Headlamps shine on it
People drive slowly through it
Creeping all around.

Matthew Bourne (9)
Crumlin High Level Primary School

Weather Haikus

Fog
Scary, slow, creeping
Slithering across the land
Darkness all around.

Lightning
Zigzag yellow stripes
Electric sparks in the sky
Zigzags pass me by.

Hail
Jumping little balls
Hard balls of bouncing ice shells
Jolly, merry, nice.

Holly Gordon (9)
Crumlin High Level Primary School

Weather Haikus

Storm
Hurricane stirring
Lightning crashing and bolting
Rain is falling down.

Snow
Falling from the trees
Sloshy, slippery and cold
Running down your neck.

Sun
Melting lush ice cream
A giant ball of hot flames
Cool off in the sea.

Rain
Running droplets form
Splishy splashy from the drains
Walk to school, no chance!

Megan Norris (9)
Crumlin High Level Primary School

Evacuees

I see them leaving home,
I see them so sad,
Leaving them alone,
They must be going mad.

I feel so sad inside,
How could they leave their mum and dad?
They probably want to hide
It's so sad.

Now they're on the train,
Leaving now.
It's starting to rain,
How could they do it, how?

Kelly-Anne Edwards (11)
Crumlin High Level Primary School

Weather Haikus

Tornado
Crashing and smashing
Raging, tearing things apart
Squashing and killing.

Snow
Falling from the sky
Pittering and pattering
Slowly touches ground.

Hail
Bouncing and jumping
Hitting the ground really hard
And it really hurts.

Storm
Blowing and throwing
Rainy droplets are falling
Lightning in the sky.

Ryan Bourne (9)
Crumlin High Level Primary School

WWII Evacuee

Children I see leaving home,
Leaving mums and dads
Don't know where to go
They want to be left alone.

Children sad
For leaving home
Every age
You could be one.

I hear children crying
Mums and dads saying
How sad they must be
So listen to me.

Emily Evans (11)
Crumlin High Level Primary School

The Dragon

She has a coat of glittering scales
Fangs as long as my arm
Claws as sharp as swords, tail a giant mace
Wingspan as wide as two buildings
Puts any bird to disgrace.

She has eyes like giant sapphire
An inferno in every breath
Can fly as high as forever
Strikes fear into the bravest soldier
And is cunning and witty and clever.

She is a faithful friend and companion
A dragon can live forever
But costs a fortune to feed
The dragon inside my heart is a valiant noble steed.

Fern Johnson (11)
Crumlin High Level Primary School

It's Chocolate Day

The shiny wrapper glistens in the light
I open it to take a big bite!
I can feel it melting in my hand
It looks so smooth, put it down, it's too grand!

I can feel the light brown texture, yum!
The purplish wrapper in the bin gone
I sit back down and think of it,
Floating down to my tummy's pit.

I can hear the crinkling wrapper,
As it gets thrown away,
I've never eaten so much chocolate
But it is Chocolate Day.

Mercedes Parry (10)
Crumlin High Level Primary School

Cool Dude

See:
>I see a motorbike
>It's going very fast
>I see it jumping through the air
>It's going very fast.

Hear:
>We can hear its engine roaring
>With a big brum, brum
>It's a KX80
>Which is very, very big.

Feel:
>I can feel the bike whizzing to one ramp
>I'm feeling very, very damp
>And extremely wet.

Alex Gingell (10)
Crumlin High Level Primary School

Shot-Put

I'm stepping up to the stand
Shot-put in my hand
Bending down to the floor
My hands start to get sore.

People with the British flag
Hoping that I win
People shouting out my name
What an amazing game.

Throw the shot-put in the air
Comes crashing to the ground
Hurrah! I win! Oh wait,
Last place is where I come.

Jake Farmer (11)
Crumlin High Level Primary School

A Walk In The Park

I can see a man walking in the park,
I can see a man walking in the dark,
I can see a boy playing on the road,
I can see a man eating a big fat toad.

I can feel the wind blowing by,
I can feel a dead, squashed fly,
I can feel a man hitting me,
I can feel a big bad bee.

I can hear a man shouting in the city,
I can hear a man shouting, 'Oh, what a pity.'
I can hear the wind blowing by,
I can hear a boy shouting the name 'Ty'.

Ryan Sayce (10)
Crumlin High Level Primary School

Sweetie Land

Oh sweeties you're a dream, like a cloud floating by,
Tastier than chocolate dreams in the sky.

Sweetie Land is a wonderful place,
Where gummy bears have a sweetie face,
Oh please don't make me cry, I love you, that's why.

Please don't make me cry and weep
Because I dream about you when I sleep.
Your fizzy sherbet, your sugared coat,
But I've only got a five pound note!

Courtney Jones (10)
Crumlin High Level Primary School

The Rugby Game

Wales beat England 11-9
England's coach gives a big whine
Wales are the best in the land
Even if the field isn't really grand.

Wales champions for 2007
They will be saints by the time they go to Heaven.
We will win the Six Nations
From all the Welsh fans a big 'Congratulations'.

Stephen Jones number 10
The Welsh team has fifteen men
Gareth Thomas the Welsh captain
Makes us win again.

Emily Thomas (11)
Crumlin High Level Primary School

We Are Playing Rugby

I can see the players working their hearts out
The other team are fighting back
The referee blowing his whistle because there is a fight.

I can feel the boot on my knee
I can feel the ruck it is really hurting me
The teams are playing really hard.

I can hear the coach shouting really loud
He is shouting, 'Really good play!
Keep it up today.'
When we won, we had a nice bun.

Alex Toms (10)
Crumlin High Level Primary School

Olympics

I am running in the 100m sprint
It is a long way to go,
Catching up to first place
Passing people that I know.

Next is the high jump
Jumping really high,
Lifting my knees
Up into the sky.

Now it's swimming
I will swim really fast,
I will win the race
It will be a blast.

Emily Leader (10)
Crumlin High Level Primary School

Inside A Forest

A forest can be big or small
A forest is a calm place
For an army base.
A forest can be scary and dark
Unlike a park
I don't care what it's like.

I still like the forest
A forest can be old or new or a play area just
For you.

I don't care what it's like
I still like the forest.

Domonic Norman (7)
Crumlin High Level Primary School

Weather Haikus

Fog
It blocks your vision
It is always in your way
It is like thick dust.

Hail
It's loud as a drum
Is like a big metal stone
Spinning off your house.

Lightning
Always on the move
It strikes among our houses
In city or town.

Rain
It falls from the sky
It is always on the go,
It sometimes forms floods.

Alyssia Ward (9)
Crumlin High Level Primary School

A Secret Forest

A forest could be scary
A forest could be dark
A forest could be big or small
A forest could be a park.

A forest could be full of trees
A forest could have bumblebees
A forest could be full of frogs
A nice place to walk your dogs.

A forest could have slithery snakes
A forest could have river lakes
A forest could have dirty rakes
But I like it.

Calwyn Fry (7)
Crumlin High Level Primary School

Football Crazy

I can see the opponents all around getting ready to take us down
Looking down at my boots covered with mud and grass
I can see the far end of the pitch as I stand by the goal.

I can feel the ball going in the back of the net
I can feel the wind blowing past me and my opponent
I can feel the skid mark in my leg
I can feel the ball slapping on my chest.

I can hear the opponents shouting, 'Come on, it's 5-4.'
I can hear the ball flying up in the air,
I can hear us shouting, 'Yes! We Won!'

Brandon Hiscox (10)
Crumlin High Level Primary School

The Forest

Trees blow wild sticks across the floor.

Insects scatter up trees.
It is dark, dirt blows everywhere.

Animals run around.
Leaves blow smoothly.
Bones are all around you.

Grass is green, bark does not move,
Colours of the forest are all around you.

Lewys James (7)
Crumlin High Level Primary School

A Forest

Today I went in the forest and saw a rat
Then I saw a fish swimming in a lake
Then I saw a mouse in a little house
Then I saw a dog on a log
Then I saw a bird trying to fly up in the sky.

Liam Edwards (7)
Crumlin High Level Primary School

In A Forest

In a forest on a cold night,
With the shining moon very bright,
With footprints on dirty paths.

Trees so big they reach the sky,
Lots of leaves fall to the ground.

Squirrels squeaking and wagging their tails all about,
As my belly is rumbling and I'm stumbling.

It's hard to find a way out at night,
Because the trees are blocking the light,

And both of my wellies are making a banging noise.

Jed Hamar-Davies (7)
Crumlin High Level Primary School

In The Forest

When it's autumn the leaves turn brown,
Red and all kinds of colours.
In the winter there are only branches on the trees,
Because there is a carpet of leaves on the ground.
You can also have fun in the forest
Because they have tree houses and tree swings.

Craig Fletcher (8)
Crumlin High Level Primary School

The Secret Forest

In the forest it is full of mud.
In the forest flowers are in bud.
Insects crawling across the ground.
Some insects make a sound.
In the forest some insects are big.
Some insects are small.

James Chivers (7)
Crumlin High Level Primary School

Haikus For The Seasons

Spring
Animals are born
Trees are growing brand new leaves
Weather is warmer.

Summer
The sun is warmer
I eat ice cream at the beach
Building sandcastles.

Autumn
Leaves are being crushed
Trees becoming bare of leaves
Hedgehogs hibernate.

Winter
Snowballs and snowmen
All the birds are flying south
Snow falls on bare trees.

Dylan John (9)
Durham Road Junior School

Season Cinquains

Winter
Chattering teeth
Tingling fingertips
I'm slipping and sliding outside
Frosty!

Summer
Happy children
Licking melting ice cream
Everyone splashing in the sea
Sun *shine!*

Jordan Pickering (8)
Durham Road Junior School

A River's Story

River
Rushing streams
Tumbling over rocks
Splashing over big boulders
Finding its way downhill.

River
Cascading down
Waterfall roaring loud
Crashing down a hill
Pouring deep down a hill.

River
Slowing down
Meandering round islands
Flowing to the sea
Taking sand and tiny rocks.

Corey Cosslett (9)
Durham Road Junior School

In The Street

Dog barking on the porch.
Houses with patterned windows.
Cars zooming past!
Children running to school.
Cats miaowing at the windows.
Babies crying in buggies.
Trains on the railway.
Motorbikes screeching.
Gutters like rotten eggs.
Dogs muck!
Salt that makes your nose twitch.
Vinegar that makes your eyes water.

Amber Bendall (7)
Durham Road Junior School

Moon Poem

The full moon shines
Like a bright round snowball
The full moon
Is like a crystal ball shining.

Watching moon gazing down
Lighting up the dark, dark town.

The crescent moon has a big smile
Like a curved boomerang,
The crescent moon
Is like a luminous glowing eyebrow.

Watching moon gazing down
Lighting up the dark, dark town.

The changing moon fading
Like a candle going out
The changing moon
Is like a dimming light bulb.

Watching moon gazing down
Lighting up the dark, dark town.

Bethan Hill-Howells (9)
Durham Road Junior School

In The Street

Shops selling food.
Some dogs running around.
See the school dogs barking.
Cats miaowing because they want to get back in their houses.
There are the traffic lights.
Dogs' mess!
More coming for pasties burning in Greggs.
Bacon smell coming from a house.

Olivia Bell (7)
Durham Road Junior School

Moon Poem

The full moon glowing
Like a reindeer's nose
The full moon beautiful
Is like a shiny clock face.

Glowing bright in the night
Making all the town so light.

The crescent moon bright and silver
Like a glittering headband
The crescent moon
Is like a curling eyebrow.

Glowing bright in the night
Making all the town so light.

The changing moon fading away
Like a small potato
The changing moon deflating away
Like a balloon.

Glowing bright in the night
Making all the town so bright.

Shorna Devney (9)
Durham Road Junior School

In The Street

Children screaming as they play
Babies sucking on their bottles
Dogs muck!
People walking nearby.
Babies crying.
Cars leading to Durham Road Junior School.
Dogs barking on the other side of the road.
Cars, petrol smelling as they are driving along.
Pancakes frying in a pan.
Children playing stuck in the mud.
Mums pushing their prams.

Lauren Russell (8)
Durham Road Junior School

Season Haikus

Winter
Frosty ice melting
Hungry birds pecking at bread
Snug by the warm fire.

Summer
Walking on the sand
Ice cream melting on the beach
Swimming in the sea.

Autumn
Squirrels saving nuts
And crispy leaves on the ground
Leafless trees swaying.

Spring
Trees are blossoming
Rabbits nibbling at the grass
Colourful flowers.

Curtis Ayling (9)
Durham Road Junior School

Special Places

I'd love to live in
A green shiny field
Full of grey and white spotted horses
With a bed made out of horses' silky skin.
I would ride a beautiful shiny horse
And say,
'I love horses.'

I'd love to live in
A yellow glittery sandcastle
With a bed made out of silky sand.
I would ride my armoured horse across the sand
And say,
'I love the beach.'

Abigail Lewis (8)
Durham Road Junior School

Special Places

I'd love to live in
A graveyard full of ghosts
With a bed made out of crunchy leaves.
I would dance with the ghostly music
And say
'It's spooky!'

I'd love to live in
A sky full of fluffy clouds
With a cloud bed.
I would fly up to the sun
And say
'It's too high up here!'

I'd love to live in
The deep blue sea
With dead shells and seaweed,
And I would play with the fish and say,
'I want to swim up to the surface!'

Eleanor Mumford (7)
Durham Road Junior School

In The Street

People driving down the road
Bins with flies flying around
Roads with white lines
Ants in the gutter carrying stones.

Motorbikes going *brmmmmm! Brmmmm!*
Dogs going *woof woof* and growling.
Cats miaowing *miaow miaow!*
Children shouting louder and louder!

Dogs muck!
Smelly eggs in nearby houses
Chips from Leo's chip shop
Ice cream from ice cream vans.

Caitlin Mazey (7)
Durham Road Junior School

Caerleon Road

I see
Birds flying in the sunny sky
People eating big chips
And cars slowing down
On Caerleon Road.

I hear
Girls shouting to get their sandwiches
Mums chatting to their friends
And birds singing in their nests
On Caerleon Road.

I smell
Chips and fish in the shop
Big cakes in the bakery
And ham sandwiches that children love
On Caerleon Road.

Katie Gregory (8)
Durham Road Junior School

Caerleon Road

I see
Mums going on the bus to town
And dads busy chatting
On Caerleon Road.

I hear
Traffic stopping at the traffic lights
Babies in the shops crying
And old people gossiping
On Caerleon Road.

I smell
Fish and chips from the chippy
Bread from the bakers
And the petrol pumps
On Caerleon Road.

Mia Frost (8)
Durham Road Junior School

Special Places

I'd love to live in
A school hall
With
A blue thick mat for my bed.
I would
Do cartwheels
And say
'Wicked! . . . Wicked!'

I'd love to live in
A dark attic
With a bed of rats inside.
I would
Run around quickly
And say
'Help! Help!'

I'd love to live in
A cornfield
With scarlet poppies for my bed.
I would
Smell the pretty flowers
And say
'Perfume, perfume!'

Morgan Roberts (7)
Durham Road Junior School

In The Street

Engine sheds
Shops selling sweets
The school
Engine diesel smelling
Smelly dogs muck
Bacon sizzling in the house
Hear steam engines
Cars beeping
People talking.

Benjamin Norvill (7)
Durham Road Junior School

Special Places

I'd love to live in
A secret mansion
With a bed made out of soft velvet.
I would run in the rose petal garden
And say
'I love it here!'

I'd love to live in
A Hawaiian ocean
With a bed of seashells.
I would swim to bed at night
And say
'This bed is uncomfortable!'

I'd love to live in
The galaxy
With a bed of
Twinkling stars.
I would explore the planets
And say
'I wonder what the weather's like below?'

I'd love to live in
A huge sweet cottage
With a bed made of candy canes.
I would eat sweets all day and night
And say
'Mmm, yummy!'

Katie Dorling (8)
Durham Road Junior School

Caerleon Road

I smell . . .
The bakery smell of cakes
Drifting through the air.
The exhaust of the cars
That travel along the road.
And sandwiches for people's lunch
On Caerleon Road.

I hear
The pelican crossing beeping.
The adults chatting to one another,
And the birds chirping on the chimneys
On Caerleon Road.

I see . . .
The busy shops full of people.
The boys riding their bikes
And babies in their buggies
On Caerleon Road.

Jack Reese (7)
Durham Road Junior School

November Poem

No ice creams dripping down babies' bibs.
No ladies walking around in bikinis.
Nobody wearing shorts and T-shirts in the sun.
Nobody going on holidays.
No children staying out late at night.
Nobody going to fairs.
Nobody going to beaches.
November.

Freddie Mears (10)
Durham Road Junior School

Caerleon Road

I see
Birds pecking at crumbs
Children going to school
And grandmas buying sweets
On Caerleon Road.

I hear
Dogs barking loud.
Toddlers screeching in the busy shops
And vans beeping their horns
On Caerleon Road.

I smell
Fish and chips from the chippy
Sausage roll smells drifting out of Greggs
And flowers on the pavement
On Caerleon Road.

Brogan Jones (8)
Durham Road Junior School

Caerleon Road

I see . . .
Cars slowing down on the road.
Birds flying in the sky
And children running in and out of shops,
On Caerleon Road.

I hear . . .
Cars beeping and revving,
Teenagers chatting to their friends
And the traffic
On Caerleon Road.

I smell . . .
Fish and chips at the chippy.
Egg sandwiches and ice cream
And perfume in the chemist
On Caerleon Road.

Isabel Reeves (7)
Durham Road Junior School

A Very Special Place

I'd love to live in
A yummy chocolate shop
With a bed made of jelly beans.
I would munch at the chair
And say
'Yum, chocolate!'

I'd love to live in
A noisy airport
With a bed made of luggage.
I would drive the planes all day
And say
'I like it here!'

I'd love to live in
A theme park
With a bed made of tickets
I would
Go on all the rides all day long
And say
'I'm safe on this ride.'

Hannah Cox (7)
Durham Road Junior School

Air Raid

Out of the placid evening sky the planes come,
Screeching down over the rooftops and the harbour
Machine guns rattle continuously,
Confused and chaotic people running for their lives
Cities being bombed everywhere,
Nazis filleting roads like the backbone of a fish.
German planes roaring across the sky,
Farm animals starting stampede in the gunfire,
Jerries filling the sky with paratroopers,
People trying to escape the deathtrap,
Screams of terror filling the air.

William Davis (10)
Durham Road Junior School

A Very Special Place

I'd love to live in
A warm blue tent
With a bed made of grass
I would watch the owls
And say, 'It's warm in here.'

I'd love to live in
A red sailing boat
With a bed made of cod
I would watch the fish swimming
And say, 'It's smelly in here.'

I'd love to live in
A mole hole
With a bed made of worms
I would watch the worms wriggling
And say, 'I'm tickling.'

Luke Orphan (8)
Durham Road Junior School

Helping Poem

Helping hands all the time,
We'll introduce our lovely rhyme.

Helping is very cool
So don't end up being a fool.

When I help people smile,
So I'll be out in a little while.

Helping is very cool
So don't end up being a fool.

Go to bed when you're told,
Then you'll be as good as gold.

Helping is very cool,
So don't end up being a fool.

Sam Williams & Luke McCarthy (9)
Durham Road Junior School

A Very Special Place

I'd love to live in
A bakery
With a bed made of soft bread,
I would
Eat gingerbread men
And say
'I like eating these.'

I'd love to live in
A rainbow
With a bed made of colourful birds' feathers,
I would
Always be colourful
And say
'I like it up here in the sky.'

I'd love to live in
A beach hut
With a bed made of sand grains and soggy seaweed,
I would
Watch the crabs scuttling by
And say
'This is great.'

Hannah Payne (7)
Durham Road Junior School

November Poem

No more ice cream dripping off the Cornish cone.
No more daffodils standing like an army of workmen.
No more sunshine hanging in the sky so high.
No more holidays when you're lying on the sandy beach.
No more rainbows filled with bright light colours.
No more barbecues heating up the juicy brown burgers.
No more sandals sinking in the sand so deep.
No more picnics on the great green grass.

Matthew Collins (11)
Durham Road Junior School

Helping Poem

We like helping we think it's fine,
We like helping all of the time.

Clear everything off your plate,
To be the dinner ladies best mate.
The mess is horrendous not at all fine,
But we clean it up all of the time.

We like helping we think it's fine,
We like helping all of the time.

We clean the pots and pans and dishes,
And feed the cat, the dog and fishes.
After I've tidied up all my stuff,
My mum gives me all the things I love.

Mark Delaney & Ben Reese (9)
Durham Road Junior School

Air Raid

All I could hear were the cries and moans,
Planes swept down from the sky,
Machine guns being lowered,
The crackling sound of fire
Then the stink of grey smoke.
A scream of terror filled the room,
Hearts were pounding,
The bombs were zigzagging in the sky,
Sometimes it was silent before being very loud,
Buildings came crashing down
Leaving many casualties,
The target is a terrible place
When countries are at war.

Katie Upton (10)
Durham Road Junior School

Jabberwocky Began

He took the horrendous eruption of the roaring volcano
The howling of the wolf
His voice was made.

He stole the colours from the glimmering rainbow
He snatched the roughness from the sand
His skin was made.

He robbed the pearly white horn from the fearless rhino
The oysters from the shimmering sea,
His teeth were created.

He stole the sharp swords from the knight in shining armour,
He took the mountains high,
His spiky back was produced.

He robbed the redness from the daring Devil,
The mighty flames from the blazing sun,
They were used for his eyes,
Jabberwocky was made.

Shannen Arnold (11)
Durham Road Junior School

November Poem

No more lounging around like a lazy orang-utan in the sun.
No more squirrels collecting chestnuts.
No calm seas like a baby sleeping soundly.
No bears running around like a speed train.
No sun-tan bottles being squeezed and squashed.
No bee stings as bright as a beetroot.
No more barbecues sizzling with hot flames like a volcano erupting.
No bikinis covering up naked tanned bodies.
November.

Cheyenne Jayne-Manning (10)
Durham Road Junior School

The Battle Of Mars

Two gigantic armies ready for battle.
They raise their guns ready,
Boom! The battle begins.

Tanks, shooting and blowing up,
Machine guns clattering, piercing hearts
Mowing men down in millions,
A slow moving river of blood.

Grenades blowing soldiers apart like fireworks exploding in the sky,
Mines buried deep and blowing tanks to smithereens,
Knives ripping flesh and skin.

Then *boom!*
A massive planet full of death
Nothing could have survived.

Alex Collins (11)
Durham Road Junior School

Air Raid

Machine guns rattle,
Soldiers battle,
People dying,
Children crying,
Screams of terror,
Guns blazing,
The terror keeps people gazing.
Planes soar
With a fiendish roar,
Collapsing buildings,
Mass destruction,
Manes of crackling flame
And Hitler and Germany are to blame.
Air raid.

Ben Reese (9)
Durham Road Junior School

Courage!

The vase had been quite pretty
Of course that was before
It fell right off the shelf
And smashed there on the floor.
'Oh what can I do now?'
Thought the little girl called Daisy,
'I suppose I'll have to tell the truth,
But Mother will go crazy!'
She gathered up all her courage,
She got herself prepared,
She knew she'd done something awful,
She really was quite scared.
Her mother did give her a lecture,
But said she wasn't so bad.
'After all,' she said, 'You did tell the truth.'
It was the best telling off Daisy'd had!

Demi Micallef (10) & Ayeshah Behit (11)
Durham Road Junior School

Courage

Courage is inside you
Courage is always there
Courage is even there
When you don't really care.

Courage makes you feel valiant,
Courage makes you feel strong
When you have courage
With you, you can do no wrong.

Courage is determination
Courage is your power
Courage gives you strength
So you don't have to cower.

Philip Dixon (10)
Durham Road Junior School

Overheard On A Saltmarsh
(Based on 'Overheard on a Saltmarsh' by Harold Munro)

'Nymph, Nymph, what are your gems?'
'Red rubies, Goblin. Why do you gaze at them?'
'Give them me.'
'No!'
'Give them me. Give them me.'
'No!'
'Then I shall screech all through the night,
Shriek like a banshee.'
'Goblin, why do you admire them so?'
'They are better than life itself,
Better than the moon and stars,
Better than the sun and water,
Your red, red rubies.'
'Hush, I stole them from the giant.'
'Give me your rubies. I need them.'
'No!'
'I will howl as loud as a werewolf
For your red, red rubies, I love them so.'
'Give them me. Give them.'
'No!'

Luke Rogers (10)
Durham Road Junior School

Air Raid

P arachuting from the sky machine gun rattling,
A re they going to shoot or will I live?
R acing out of the way of angry men firing,
A bomb explodes at my feet giving a huge shock,
C ord not working, panicking now,
H urrying to the ground, falling quicker and quicker,
U p, up, up the palls of smoke roll up from the harbour,
T orturing - men on the ground shouting and ready to pounce.
E very plane's propellers or wings falling from the sky.

Sam Orphan (9)
Durham Road Junior School

Mars The Planet Of War

Mars is the planet of war.
There's war all year long.
There's war here and there.
Mars is a planet full of death.

Mars is the planet of war.
Great armies driven by hate
March across the dusty, barren landscape.
A poisonous hate burning in their eyes.

War has begun on Mars.
The armies like a sea of black,
Stretching for miles and miles.
The armies shout and scream.
Battle begins.

Rockets and bullets whizz around.
Explosions everywhere.
Killing people over and over.
Finally the war stops.
Mars is peaceful . . .
For now.

Dominic Little (10)
Durham Road Junior School

Christmas

C andles flickering in the night,
H ouses lit up with twinkling lights.
R eindeer galloping over the rooftops.
I cicles hanging from snowy porches
S nowballs thrown at cars.
T reats argued over by children.
M istletoe hung up so you are kissed.
A ntlers worn by adults!
S o now my story's ended.
    Merry Christmas
        And a happy New Year!

Jessie Harrhy (10)
Durham Road Junior School

Planet War

Two armies ready for war,
They get closer,
Hearts pounding.

Mars, planet of war.

They pull out their swords,
Grab their shields,
The battle begins.

Mars, planet of war.

Swords clashing,
Guns fire,
Shields breaking.

Mars, planet of war.

Rivers of blood,
Piles of dead bodies,
Broken weapons.

Mars, planet of war.

Only the remaining alive men,
Make an escape,
Nightmares ending.

Mars, planet of war . . .
Destroyed!

Kristy Griffiths (11)
Durham Road Junior School

Skeleton

B ones bleached in vinegar
O ld bones creaking in the darkness
N othing but rot and bones
E yes just like holes
S keleton sneaking in the dark
    A creaking sound from the bones.

Sophie Challenger (8)
Durham Road Junior School

Until I Saw The Sea

Until I saw the sea,
I did not know,
That wind
Could wrinkle water so.

I never knew,
That sun
Could splinter a whole sea of blue.

Nor,
Did I know before,
A sea breathes in and out,
Upon a shore.

I never knew,
That the sea,
Could pounce,
Upon a shore.

Nor,
Did I know the
Sea could be as
Destructive as man.

Joshua Burrows (10)
Durham Road Junior School

November Poem

No women walking round in brightly coloured bikinis.
No more fun holidays in the cooling pool.
No more children running madly around in the garden.
No more ice cream running down babies chins.
No more collecting colourful shells on the blazing beach.
No more dogs sticking their big wet tongues out.
No more boys wearing sporty shorts.
No more chocolate melting quickly on the windowsill.
November.

Bethan Jones (10)
Durham Road Junior School

Overheard On A Saltmarsh
(Based on 'Overheard on a Saltmarsh' by Harold Munro)

'Pixie, Pixie, what is your crown?'
'Pure gold dwarf. Why do you gape at it?'
'Give it here.'
'No!'
'Give it here, give it me!'
'No!'
'Then I shall shriek at the night sky!
Until you give it me, give it me.'
'No!'
'Dwarf, why do you admire it so?'
'It is better than crystals, reflecting the sun's glare,
Better than the twinkling stars,
Better than the silvery moon.'
'Your supreme gold crown over rules even the sun!'
'Give it me I admire it so, give it me!'
'No!'

Jack Lapthorn (10)
Durham Road Junior School

November Poem

No ice creams dripping to make a creamy river on the pavement.
No barbecue on a nice sunny day.
No going to the fairground to enjoy the rides.
No more hot summer days.
No building sandcastles on the beach.
No swimming in the back garden.
No sunbathing to get a nice tan.
No more wearing sandals in the hot weather.
No more wearing shorts in the sun.
November.

Jordan Kemp (10)
Durham Road Junior School

Overheard On A Salt Mountain
(Based on 'Overheard on a Saltmarsh' by Harold Monro)

'Nymph, nymph, what are your diamonds?'
'Green glass, goblin. Why do you want them so?'
'Give them to me.'
'No!'
'Give them to me. Give them to me.'
'No!'
'Then I will howl all night in the bushes and the reeds,
Lie in the water and shout for them.'
'Goblin why do you like them so?'
'They are better than the planets and the solar system,
They are better than the sun and moon.'
'I stole them from space.'
'Give me your diamonds, I want them.'
'No!'
'I will scream in a deep pond and I won't go away.'
'Give them to me.'
'I love them so,'
'Give them to me. Give them.'
'No!'

James Ford (10)
Durham Road Junior School

November Poems

No more ice cream dripping down hands and onto the floor.
No swimming pools in the gardens with people splashing around.
No more hot burning sun in the sky.
No more sheep having lambs in the fields.
No more sunbathing getting suntans.
No more sandcastles in the sand on the beaches.
No more blossom falling from the trees onto the ground.

Samantha Reeves (10)
Durham Road Junior School

Wind Song

When the wind blows
The quiet things sing.
Some bang, some bash,
Some even ping.

Bushes rock
Sheds creak
Branches tilt
To take a peek.
Doors cry
Like my cat,
Floorboards whistle
Raindrops pat.

When the wind fades,
The noises drop,
Leaving me
To sleep non-stop.

Jessica Haggerty (11)
Durham Road Junior School

Peacock's Feathers

A peacock's feather dancing in the breeze
A comet rushing through space
Its big eye staring at you
A beautiful green metallic eyelash
Its tendrils like tentacles
A prize in a treasure chest
Its eye like a purple shroud
A gem for an eye
Its long stem bright white
A relic of beauty.

Morgan Hoskins (8)
Durham Road Junior School

Wind Song

When the wind blows
The quiet things speak.
Some whisper, some clang,
Some creak.

Doors slam!
Dustbins chatter
Branches hit a window
With a sudden clatter.

Park swings squeak,
Plastic bags crackle.
The wind makes wind chimes
Move and rattle.

After all that,
When the wind goes
Where are all the noises?
Everyone knows.

Jennifer Murphy (11)
Durham Road Junior School

The Giant Wave

A witch's nail snapping
A sharp icicle dripping
A cat catching a mouse
A shark opening its sharp jaw
A ghostly figure
Icy dungeons
A huge waterfall about to crash
Who woke the dragon from its sleep?

Hope Merrick (8)
Durham Road Junior School

War On Planet Mars

Mars is a rusty planet
Bright red like the sun,
The monster released and war has begun.
Soldier against soldier,
Fighting for their lives,
With guns and sharp knives.

Bang! Bang! The guns go,
Shooting people off their toes,
Bang! Bang! Bang!

People dying on the ground,
Crying for help,
But no one hears the sound.

Soldiers still fighting to rule planet Mars,
We will not stop fighting until we win,
Soldiers shouting out loud. Bang!

Soldiers screaming when they are shot,
There is a giant bomb,
Bang!

There is no more fighting,
No guns, nothing,
War is no more on planet Mars.

Emily Langford (10)
Durham Road Junior School

November Poem

No more ice creams dripping on the ground.
No more daisies smelling beautiful.
No more Dax topless men dancing on the beach.
No more blackberries growing on the branches.
No more barbecues on a hot summer day.
No more tans out on the beach.

Timothy Berrow (10)
Durham Road Junior School

The Moon

The full moon sparkles
Like a queen's orb sitting in her hand.
The full moon,
Is like a silver bundle of knitting wool.

Watching moon gazing down
Lighting up things all over the town.

The crescent moon is soggy,
Like a sweet slice of melon.
The crescent moon,
Is like a baby's cot swaying.

Watching moon, gazing down
Lighting up things all over the town.

The changing moon bumps
Like an old shrivelled potato.
The changing moon
Is like a bursting bubble popping.

Megan Davies (8)
Durham Road Junior School

Rocket Ride

Rocket racing round and round
Orbiting around the world
Knuckles going whiter and whiter
Entertaining lights flashing on and off
Twisting and turning up and down.

Riding rocket faster and faster
Invisible people down below
Dizzy and desperate to get off
End of the rocket ride.

Rory Mitchell (9)
Durham Road Junior School

Christmas

C hestnuts roasting on an open fire
H ear the church bells ringing happily
R eindeer flying high in the sky
I ce rinks with skaters all around
S tars glimmering, waiting for Santa to come
T oys all wrapped up under the tree
M ums and dads rushing for time
A merry Christmas to you all
S anta says, 'Ho! Ho! Ho! Ho!'

Danielle Sharpe (9)
Durham Road Junior School

Skeleton

B uried deep in a stony graveyard
O nly bones left in the coffin
N o flesh left on the body
E ye sockets hollow and staring
S kull cold like marble
    A skeleton has no feelings or soul.

Isobel Bayley (8)
Durham Road Junior School

Skeleton

B uried deep in a stony graveyard
O nly bones left in the coffin
N o flesh left on the body
E ye sockets hollow and staring
S kull cold like marble
    A skeleton sleeping forever.

Jessica Griffiths (8)
Durham Road Junior School

A Peacock's Feathers

A tiger watching its prey ready to pounce.
A galaxy full of tendrils opening up
Like a drooping branch on a tree.
A beautiful hand full of coiling ivy
Like a zooming and flashing star.
A long pole made of plastic and hairs.
Enormous black holes sucking everything in,
Like a huge duster.
Seaweed skipping and sliding up and down.
Green eyes except no eyelashes.

Jusef Behit (9)
Durham Road Junior School

Christmas

C hristmas candles bring peace and light,
H ats and scarves keep children warm,
R eindeer flying in the night,
I nvisible air whistling on Christmas Day,
S anta bringing special things,
T ables to put Christmas dinners on,
M ums and dads give you presents too,
A ll along mums and dads are the best thing,
S ugar sweet food help you live for Christmas.

Dorian Payne (9)
Durham Road Junior School

Skeleton

B are shiny bones in a grave
O ld buried bones for eternity
N o flesh left on the body
E yes, nothing left except sockets
S taring up wishing he was alive.
    A skeleton wanting his revenge.

Isabel Broadribb (8)
Durham Road Junior School

The Moon

The full moon shines
Like a silver coin.
The full moon
Is like a melting snowball.

A silver orb gleaming bright
Shining slowly through the night.

The crescent moon waves
Like a hammock in the sky,
The crescent moon
Is like an orange ready to eat.

A silver orb gleaming bright,
Shining slowly through the night.

The changing moon shrinks
Like a pufferfish
The changing moon
Is like a shrinking balloon.

Joseph Brown (8)
Durham Road Junior School

A Peacock's Feather

A peacock's feather is a long feather pen.
The eye gleams like the autumn sun.
A dancer in a green dress dancing on the stage.
Long, shooting, shining, firework.
A thin skeleton's white spine.
Icicles swaying in the breeze.
A peacock's eye is turquoise, gold and green and purple.
Shaft is soft like a polar bear's coat,
And tendrils like a cornfield swaying in the breeze.

Olivia Gregory (9)
Durham Road Junior School

The Moon

The full moon shines like a round new handle,
The full moon is like a silver orb.

A silver orb gleaming bright,
Shining always in the night.

The crescent moon laughs,
Like a happy smile.
The crescent moon
Is like a thick eyebrow.

A silver orb gleaming bright
Shining always in the night.

The changing moon shrinks
Like an old ball being kicked.
The changing moon
Is like a shrivelled old potato.

Bethan Porter (9)
Durham Road Junior School

The Moon

The full moon shines like a slice of melon.
The full moon is like a ball of silver knitting wool.

Glowing bright in the night,
Flashing slowly, what a sight.

The crescent moon sways
Like a hammock high in the sky.
The crescent moon is like a banana cradle rocking.

A silver orb gleaming bright
Shining high in the sky at night.

The changing moon shrinks like an old potato shrivelled.
The changing moon is like a cold person sneezing.

Watching moon gazing down
Wearing a wondrous silver crown.

Tinotenda Nyamunda (9)
Durham Road Junior School

The Moon

The full moon shines like a silver skull.
The full moon is like a barn owl perched in a tree.

A silver orb gleaming bright
What a lovely glowing sight.

The crescent moon sparkles like a queen's long cloak.
The crescent moon is like a happy smile.

A silver orb gleaming bright
What a lovely glowing sight.

The changing moon grows like an ageing child.
The changing moon is like a melting ice cube.

Jarrod Lewis (9)
Durham Road Junior School

The Giant Wave

A winter dragon roaring in anger,
A waterfall cascading over rocks,
A vanilla ice cream dripping on the floor,
Whales' flukes whipping waves,
Witches' spiky fingers poking people.
A snow-topped mountain with frilly edges.
A huge giant stamping in a puddle.

Who woke the winter dragon up?

Amber Howell (8)
Durham Road Junior School

A Peacock's Feather

One hundred and fifty feathers lullabying you to sleep.
A bomb that blows a great big smile on your face.
A gleaming eye looking closely.
The London Eye going around and around.
An ordinary peacock is its name.

Jack Masters (9)
Durham Road Junior School

A Peacock's Feather

A waxy white demon with a million arms.
A chameleon camouflaged among one thousand antennas.
A new improved backscratcher.
The colours of a mint green bouncy ball.
The shaft is like a bright glowing shooting star.
My mind's eye using up all of its glamorous powers.
A crystal clear view that you never expected to see.
A metallic wave flowing in the breeze.
A flower blooming in the sun.
A mysterious spy reaching up high.
The most colourful rainbow ever.
A weird looking swan swimming gracefully.

Johnny Sheeran (8)
Durham Road Junior School

The Giant Wave

A hippo's mouth opening.
A wizard's cloak swaying in the breeze.
The rain crashing down on the sea.
A blue blanket covering the sea.
A dragon's tongue curving to eat its prey.
A giant's foot ready to crush boats.
    Who spilled the wizard's potion?

Ellie Hopkins (8)
Durham Road Junior School

Peacock's Feather

A mint-green explosion darting out of a black hole.
An antenna as long as a metre ruler.
A centipede scurrying through the dead grass.
The shaft as furry and as white and as fluffy as my grandpa's hair.
A one hundred-legged ghoulie monster.

Oliver Dowie (8)
Durham Road Junior School

The Moon

The full moon shines like a gleaming but wrinkly lemon.
The full moon is like a freezing cold snowball.

Glowing bright in the night
Flashing slowly, what a sight.

The crescent moon glowing like a silver banana with pointy edges.
The crescent moon is like a very happy clown's smile.

Watching moon, gazing down
Shining bright like a clown.

The changing moon shrinking like a shrivelled potato.
The changing moon is like a silver balloon.

Harvey Abraham-Evans (8)
Durham Road Junior School

A Peacock's Feather

Its feathers are like glittering rainbows sparkling up in the sky.
Its shaft is as white as gleaming teeth.
It makes me feel good.
To some people scared because of its shadow.
Its colours are blue, turquoise, fluorescent green and black.
It sways from side to side.
Gracefully moving.

Jake Abraham (8)
Durham Road Junior School

A Peacock's Feather

A peacock's feather is graceful, as graceful as the calm sea.
A peacock's feather looks like a hole, a great dark hole.
The peacock's shaft looks like the white wizard's staff.
A peacock's feathers are blue, as blue as a ballerina's beautiful tutu.
A peacock's feather is colourful, turquoise, blue, purple and green.

Stephanie England (9)
Durham Road Junior School

Christmas

Iced top red and white cake,
On the table ready to take,
Christmas crackers with an awesome treat,
Mince pies for Santa Claus to eat,
Reindeer outside, they're a bore,
While Santa is sleeping behind a door,
Tinsel, chocolate decorations,
Cake, Christmas celebrations,
A green tree in the breeze,
And people while they sleep they sneeze,
Chocolate Shrek and doll calendars,
Outside are sleeping reindeer,
Santa is ready for the big day,
But his reindeer are hibernating, so they say,
Christmas trees glow in the night,
Still a red nose is shining bright,
Santa is going to his sledge for a big night,
But his reindeer are still asleep tucked in tight.

Ben Heath (9)
Durham Road Junior School

A Peacock's Feather

A peacock's feather swaying back and forth
Like a feather pen showing off.
An eyelash straight and tall
Like a centipede crawling around.
A blazing hot firework
Like a spinning disco ball.
A flashing glass ball on the green Christmas tree,
Like a fairy's wing flying high.
A giant monster with a thousand legs like the deep blue sea,
Bobbing up and down.
The skeleton's back spine with veins coming out.
The glowing light of a comet with yellow and orange sparks.

Rebecca Farley (9)
Durham Road Junior School

In The Street

Children screaming as they play-fight.
Babies sucking their favourite bottles.
Cars zooming down the road.
Dogs bouncing to catch their sticks.
Roads leading to Durham Road School.
Boys playing footie on the way to school.
Children laughing to the bitter end.
Music springing out of the car stereo.
Cats scratching at the front door.
Dog's muck! *(yuck!)*
Yucky burgers!
Chips from the fish and chip shop.
Car petrol that reeks!
Everybody in the street is very happy.

Rebecca Taylor (8)
Durham Road Junior School

In The Street

Children chasing down the street.
Mums pushing prams.
Babies learning to walk.
A baby crying.
Mums talking.
Cars going past.
Dogs barking wildly.
A rough wall.
Smooth floor.
Dog's muck on my shoe!
A cat scratching my hand.
In the street.

Andrew Sprudd (8)
Durham Road Junior School

In The Street

Rubbish scattered all over the street.
Bins pushed over.
Traffic lights going red, orange and green.
Roads with yellow lines.
People talking away.
Children laughing out loud.
Motorbikes revving their engines.
Trains chugging on the railway
Dog's muck smelling.
Burgers stinking from shops.
Cars' exhausts reeking.
Bacon cooking from a nearby house.

Joe Palmer-Phillips (8)
Durham Road Junior School

In The Street

Dogs chase cats all through the day.
The café full of people eating.
Traffic lights changing from red to yellow to green.
People rushing to their business jobs.
Sirens making whirring sounds.
Motorbikes go zoom! Zoom! Zoom!
Trains chugging on the railway lines.
Music booming from the stereo.
Chips frying in a pan.
Bacon cooking inside a house.
Dog's muck.
Roast potatoes roasting, so hot!

Bradley Bushell (8)
Durham Road Junior School

My Recipe For A Perfect World

Four teaspoons of peace to crush all wars
A cup of clean water to stop the disease
Share all money, don't spend it on weapons
Homes for the homeless and food for the poor
A bucket of luck so children can find their families
No more teasing about people who are different to us
A jar full of respect for our elders and friends
A bottle of medicine to cure cancer
Help the hurt to heal their wounds
And help the lost to find their way.

Hannah Victoria Snelling (10)
Gaer Junior School

Recipe For A Perfect World

Five cups of love to stop world hunger.
Two spoons of peace to stop the suffering.
A school of hearts to stop the cruelty of children.
No drugs or cigarettes to make people sick.
A cure for cancer and people getting hit.
Don't make fun of other people just for their skin.
Help stop bullying in other countries around the world.
That's my recipe for a perfect world.

Alexandra Blackley (10)
Gaer Junior School

A Good World

Twenty big rocks to destroy all the wars in the world.
Ten spoonfuls of sugar to stop illnesses.
Eight large houses for the homeless.
Three buckets of blood to save lives.
One mighty ocean to wash away the sad faces.
One million hands to make the world a better *place!*

Matthew Thorn
Gaer Junior School

A Vision Of Hell

A lot of disgusting, killer germs
and gruesome diseases swarm the working city
claiming angry victims every minute in Victorian England.

V ermin scuttle round the city creating a vision of Hell
as they spread their deadly germs.

I ntense nerves run wild in the dangerous, rusty factories
and dirty mines.

S everal children swarm the stinking streets
looking for somebody to love them.

I rresistible money drives the thieves to the extreme level.

O ne house is virtually stuck to another one
and the smell of the court spreads diseases.

N ight-time gales blow through the already shattered panes
of windows.

O f every baby that lives another horribly dies
leaving the mother weeping forcefully in her bedspread.

F alling rocks endanger the lives of the miners underground
as they scrape and scrape the smoky black walls.

H ateful diseases like cholera and TB claim many helpless lives
each day.

E xtravagant pain drives through the unlucky person
who has an accident in the mines.

L ife gets cut extremely short when you get infected
by a life-threatening disease.

L ucky people in the Victorian times lived up to 86 years old
compared to today's 123 years old.

Jamie Reed (11)
Gaer Junior School

My Recipe For A Perfect World

A jug of respect to keep people respecting our plants
And creatures big and small.
Don't pollute our world.
Stop smoking, littering and dumping toxic waste
In our beautiful oceans and on lands.
Three spoonfuls of love to stop all wars
And fighting all around our world.
We could save billions of lives.
Also to stop world hunger, people cutting down forests,
Poaching, hunting and extinction of our beautiful creatures.

Lauren Hillier (10)
Gaer Junior School

Recipe For A Happy 2005

I will put a stop to any more world wars,
And stop cruelty to animals.
Six spoonfuls of money to give to the poor people.
Eight shoes full of peace to stop people selling dangerous weapons
That can hurt people.
Two cups of energy for people to stop smoking to live much longer.
Stop people buying drugs for the world to be a nicer place.
Eight cupboards full of luck so there will be no more earthquakes.
Forty fighting programs to help people fight cancer.
Ten pots of money to give to the unwealthy people in this world.

Annalize James (11)
Gaer Junior School

My Recipe For A Perfect 2005

A cup of water to wash away the anger and hatred.
A wall of goodness to block out the pain.
Three spoons of joy to forgive and forget.
A jar of good memories to replace the bad ones.
It's inside that counts not what is outside.

Matthew Perrin (11)
Gaer Junior School

Recipe For A Perfect World

Five teaspoons of geniuses to stop illnesses.
A cupboard of money for Africa not for drugs.
A jar of protesters to save the rainforest.
Another jar of protesters to stop cruelty to animals.
Some more teaspoons, this time ten of helpers
And shelters for the homeless.
Finally add a large saucepan of love and kindness
And another of courage and leadership,
Then bake for ten years to get a perfect world.

Fedor Tot (11)
Gaer Junior School

The Sea Creatures

An octopus swirls his bendy tentacles
A fish has some colourful fins
A shark has terrifying teeth
A whale has a big mouth
A sea anemone does not do anything
A squid has jet propulsion
A seal has long flippers
And a jellyfish has long legs.

Rhys John Harries (9)
Gaer Junior School

A Chocolate Easter

A basketful of coloured eggs.
A time when Jesus rose again.
A time when we share our Easter eggs.
A time when all your family comes to visit.
A time when all our friends all come together.
A time when we all think about Jesus.

Anna Corten (10)
Gaer Junior School

A Vision Of Hell

A lot of people are dying

V ermin round every corner
I n dark, little holes the animals hide
S loppy mud supposed to be water
I llness spreading all around town
O ne child gets up at 5am to work
N ot a lot of children see their parents

O nly rich people can see the doctor
F or working 1 week people earn 1 shilling

'H elp us!' the children cry
E veryone has to go to a pump to get water
L ots of children cry for a home
L et's all think about a vision of Hell.

Katie Heard (10)
Gaer Junior School

Daydreaming Animals

I want to be the mighty jaguar
Prowling through the night!
I want to be a bird of prey
Flying through the light.
I want to be a mad wolf
Creeping out of sight.

I want to be an owl all feathery.
I want to be a winter fox all warm and weathery!
I want to be the sly black cat because she is all clevery.

Or I want to be an animal researcher,
Think of all the animals I could see
Yes, that's what I want to be!

Cherie Crighton (8)
Gaer Junior School

A Vision Of Hell

A disgusting, vile time to live in was the Victorian times.

V ermin in every nook with cold, damp conditions to live in.
I ll people with cholera and TB dying all around.
S preading diseases takes people's lives.
I n coal mines and factories people worked long hours.
O nly wealthy people could afford the everyday things.
N ot many people could afford food.

O ften there was no clean water.
F ilthy people begging for money.

H orrible smells from the streets and rivers
where people put their garbage.
E ven though the Queen was powerful
their lives were still miserable.
L ife was bad but there were fun times.
L ucky to live 17 years.

Mark Goddard (11)
Gaer Junior School

My Recipe For A Perfect World

Ten bags of happiness will brighten up the day
Because the war has gone away
Nine bags of caring will help the homeless have shelter
All through the day
Eight spoons of sugar to scare the illnesses away
Seven bowls of lovely foods will help poor people
All along the way
Six tubs of water pistols replacing all guns
Five bottles of helpfulness can stop people littering
Four pairs of handcuffs to stop racism
Three bags of money will help ill people get better today
Two big buckets of water to wash way the graffiti
One massive ocean will wash away the bullies.

James Morgan (11)
Gaer Junior School

A Vision Of Hell

A vision of Hell is what they say.

V ery nasty conditions to live in, especially when there is smallpox going round.
I t is disgusting because of the refuse in the streets everyone
S ays. I personally think
I t is revolting.
O h dear, they will lead horrible lives.
N o! I will never want to live there.

O nly some people seem happy.
F or goodness sake tidy yourselves up a bit!

H elpless people fighting and thieving.
E verybody is down in the dumps (apart from the rich).
L ots of refuse and sewage everywhere.
L ots of unlucky people, young and old, died every day.

Amy Turner (10)
Gaer Junior School

I Want To Be A Stone Geologist

I want to be a stone geologist
And never, ever moan
I want to be a stone geologist
And find a gallon of Portland stone.

I want to be a stone geologist
And never get hurt by a gush of thistle
I want to be a stone geologist
And discover a mine of crystal.

Dean McDonald (9)
Gaer Junior School

My Dog

My dog is brown and white
My dog has big, brown eyes
My dog is scruffy and fluffy
My dog is sooooo naughty.

My dog snores at night
My dog dreams at night
My dog loves to play
My dog is the best thing in life.

Luke Johnson (9)
Gaer Junior School

I Want To Be A Footballer

I want to be a footballer,
And score tons of goals,
I want to play for anyone,
And be better than Paul Scholes.

I want to be a striker,
And be in the Liverpool story,
I want to be at the top of the League,
And claim all the glory.

Ben Ford Weaver (8)
Gaer Junior School

Boys And Girls

Football crazy, chocolate mad!
Girls are boring and boys are mad!
Boys are dirty, girls are clean
Girls are nice and boys are mean.
Girls like make-up, boys like sport
When we play tag, the girls get caught!

Thomas Sayce-Upton (10)
Gaer Junior School

10 Things Found In Thierry Henry's Pocket

A mini football
An Arsenal shirt
A French shirt
A pair of boots
A bag of kits
A jar of skills
A ball of mud
A bottle of water
A packet of studs
A field of pitches.

Curtis Macias (10)
Gaer Junior School

10 Things Found In A Clown's Pocket

A smiley face
A bike horn
A pair of stilts
A make-up kit
A funny wig
An over-sized hat
A litre of fire
A crossed pair of eyes
A bag of people
A lion tamer.

Abigail Emily Coe (9)
Gaer Junior School

10 Things Found In My Pocket

A wrestler's belt.
A piece of jelly bean.
An Xbox and games.
A piece of cat hair.
A big feather.
A torch.
A bee sting.
A rubber band.
A pile of cards.
A five pence piece.

Jack Evans (9)
Gaer Junior School

10 Things Found In My Pocket

A PS2
A Game Boy
A box of Lego
A TV
A CD
A Simpson's toy
A video
A DVD player
A football
Some 50-pound notes.

Joshua Dominic Bertie (9)
Gaer Junior School

I Want To Be A Bird

I want to be a bird
And fly up to the clouds
And explore the world
I would be very proud.

I want to be a bird
And see all the stars
And see the shiny moon
And land on top of cars.

Kyle McCarthy (8)
Gaer Junior School

My Flower Poem

A red-coloured rose
A blossom, a pose
A white daisy, a buttercup
A butterfly that flutters up
A sweet, tender blossom
A cuddly little possum
A bluebird in the sky
A sparkle of tender flutterby.

Adrienne Bartlett (9)
Gaer Junior School

8 Things Found In My Brother's Pocket

A fish
A mobile phone
A hat
A pot of gel
A pen
A battery
A package of games
A PS2.

Hannah Louise Morgan (9)
Gaer Junior School

I Want To Be A Footballer

I want to be a footballer
And call myself Jay
And when I stick it through his legs
I'll just say, *'Olé!'*

I want to be a footballer
And make lots of money
And when I go home for tea
I'll still eat a huge jar of honey!

James Luckett (8)
Gaer Junior School

Hazell's Wood
(Based on 'Danny, Champion Of The World')

Down in the dark woods
I can see . . .
Brown dead leaves falling calmly,
Bushy squirrels eating loudly,
Furry bats swooping scarily,
A big, round, silver moon shining brightly,
A calm river flowing nicely,
And white big rats running quickly.

Down in the dark woods
I can hear . . .
Fat owls hooting wearily,
Farmers' shotguns banging distinctly,
Falling twigs snapping frighteningly,
Moaning wolves whining horribly,
Loud winds howling sluggishly
And invisible ghosts screeching fearlessly.

Emily O'Dwyer & Ryan Lewis (10)
Gorseinon Junior School

Our Environment

Stop cutting down trees,
Stop using CFCs.

Too much rain,
Too much pain.

Here comes the flood,
Bringing all the mud.

Watch out for the storm,
The people are forlorn.

Watch out for the flood,
Too much mud and blood!

Turn off the CD player,
It will damage the ozone layer!

Jack Seaward (7)
Gorseinon Junior School

Our Environment

Think of a world with floods!

Carbon dioxide and CFCs,
Killing animals, cutting down trees!

Don't destroy the ozone layer,
Please turn off the DVD player!

Please turn off the light,
The sun rays are getting too bright.

There'll soon be a great big hole,
You'll be sorry in your soul.

Look at our world, it's a mess!
We wish we could make our world a success!

Steven Jones (7)
Gorseinon Junior School

Hazell's Wood
(Based on 'Danny, Champion Of The World')

Down in the dark woods I can see . . .
Frightening black bats swooping swiftly,
Brown crunchy leaves falling gently,
Bushy red squirrels eating crunchily,
Fat grey rats running quickly,
A shallow bubbling river flowing calmly,
And a big bright moon shining dazzlingly.

Down in the dark woods I can hear . . .
Hungry wolves whining mightily,
Slow, creepy footsteps crunching gently,
Fierce winds howling thunderously,
Angry ghosts screeching horridly,
Delicate twigs snapping suddenly,
And dangerous shotguns banging tremendously.

David Davies & Jordan Yemm (10)
Gorseinon Junior School

Our Environment

Stop cutting down trees and -
By the way -
You're using too many
CFCs!

Oh for goodness sake, switch off your light!
It will damage the ozone layer and the world will be too bright.

It will cause a flood,
Everything will be covered in mud!

You call technology a success -
We've made our world a terrible mess!

Let's work together and make our world better!

Ben Davies (7)
Gorseinon Junior School

The School Trip

A nnounced a school trip
B ounced about the place in excitement
C arried his delicious packed lunch
D arted around the revving bus
E ntered the endless M4
F ound that they were lost
G asped in horror
H urried off the bus to find directions
I nterrupted the stressed teacher
J umped for joy when Castell Henllys was found
K ept himself calm as he travelled back through time
L ooked at the wonderful handcrafted Celtic round houses
M ade mouth-watering doughty bread rolls
N eeded help to plait and weave her willow basket
O pened his tasty meal
P opped his bubbly fizzy drink
Q uestioned the fearsome Celtic warrior
R ushed out of the smoky hut
S lithered about in the squelchy mud
T ossed a golden torch around the hill fort
U shered the exhausted children back onto the rattling bus
V entured home
W hined and complained of stomach ache
X -ray eyes spotted the school
Y awned with sleepiness, happy to be back
Z ipped home speedily, full of joyful memories.

Class Y6D (10)
Gorseinon Junior School

Our Environment

Why is it us?

Why are we destroying our world so quick?
Cutting down trees and using oil slicks?

Why are we using too much light?
Keep it up, the sun will be too bright!

Watch out for global warming!
Don't be smart, watch the warning!

Turn of your CD player -
You'll damage the ozone layer!

Dafydd Thomas (7)
Gorseinon Junior School

A Dog

A lovely, sweet brownie.
A sparkling jewel for an eye.
A marathon runner.
A little teddy bear.
A big barrel.
A lazy elephant.
A groggy giant.
A beautiful dog.

Rowan Joseph-Lake
Llangiwg Primary School

What Is Rain?

Its giants in their showers,
It's Mary watering her flowers,
It's God when he cries,
It's little petals falling in sunset skies,
A dripping pipe up in Heaven.

Zoe Jagoe-Williams
Llangiwg Primary School

My Cat

I have a cat
Its name is Mr T
Wherever I go
He likes to follow me.

He likes to go outside
To see all the other cats
And whenever he is bored
He likes to catch the rats.

He always likes to have a fuss
When I'm always there
And when he's in a playful mood
He likes to scratch my hair.

Annie Hughes (10)
Llangiwg Primary School

A Poem About My Family

My family always cares,
My cousins always share.
My mum might shout,
Sometimes I don't know what about.
My dad isn't as strict as my mum,
He can be quite fun.
My sister I sometimes hate,
But she can act like a mate.

Kate Thomas
Llangiwg Primary School

What Are Trees?

Trees help us live.
Give oxygen
To breathe.
It's a home for animals.

Nathan Blackler
Llangiwg Primary School

Young Writers - Playground Poets South Wales

Bonfire Night

Today it is Bonfire Night
Sometimes it gives me a big fright
Now that it's Bonfire Night.

When I see fireworks in the sky
They look so nice
How beautiful and bright they look in my eyes.

How colourful they make the sky
It makes me think I'm in Heaven
The way God makes it look.

Catherine wheels, rockets
Just the way I like
Spinning and exploding in the lovely night sky.

All the colours in the town
Spinning and dancing all around
It's the loveliest sight in the world.

Valmai Dearden (8)
Millbrook Junior School

The Sun Is A Powerful King

The sun is a powerful king
Rules the land
Tells the rain when to fall
Sits on his mighty throne keeping his gold
He is ruler of the Earth.

The sun is a powerful king
He is evil beyond compare
The clouds are his slaves.

Anthony Lloyd (11)
Millbrook Junior School

The Wallowy Depths Of The Sea

Under the sea are creaking boats,
Blue and deep and frightening
Lie skeletons, ships, plates, cups . . .
And bodies that were alive.
Slimy seaweed sways among the jewels and gold.

Broken bones and swimming souls
Are haunting all the treasure.
Broken hearts, atop the sea
For those who have been lost.

Forgotten ships, forgotten belongings
Are lost forever at sea.
Underneath the cold, wet water bodies shall lay
While on the surface you can hear funeral bells ring at the church.
Treasure lies and men's bodies lay in broken ships
All wrecked and ruined,
Stones afloat in fishes' stomachs
Wallowing sorrows atop the sea.

Katie Colborne (11)
Millbrook Junior School

Untitled

January is getting colder and Andi-Lee is one year older.
February - Valentine's Day comes and you give your love away.
March is St David's Day and you sing your little hearts out.
April we trick on people and make them laugh the whole day long.
May is joy, it's holiday joy.
June - summer is here and daffodils start popping up their heads.
July - school is shutting down and I'm going on holiday.
August is still holidays, it's nearly over.
September - we go back to school and do work all day.
October - get ready for Christmas and wrap the presents up.
November is Bonfire Night and they are very noisy,
December - it's Christmas and presents!

Alura Devlin (7)
Millbrook Junior School

The Ice Palace

Ivan lived in a pine forest full of wolves and bears
Starjik takes all the children, Ivan's brother was one of them
Brothers never more shall part
Melt the winter in his heart.

Ivan went on a quest to save his brother
Ivan went into the forest to save his lovely brother
Brothers never more shall part
Melt the winter in his heart.

Ivan was walking in the forest
He saw the wolves and froze
Brothers never more shall part
Melt the winter in his heart.

Ivan found his brother
There the tears in Starjik's face
Brothers never more shall part
Melt the winter in his heart.

Starjik was not evil
He let the children free
He fed them with soup
He left presents by their beds every year
Brothers never more shall part
Melt the winter in his heart.

Luke Morgan (10)
Millbrook Junior School

Tree Haiku

Very wise old man
Holds knowledge from years gone by
Lives and dies proudly.

Alexander William Leighton (11)
Millbrook Junior School

The Ice Palace

Ivan lived in the pine wood,
Where winter wasn't so good.
Ivan woke up one morning and had a fright,
His little brother was not in sight.

He sets on a long and tiring quest
Ivan really needed a rest
He built a warm snowdrift
Which was an excellent gift
Did Ivan save his brother?

Ivan was chased by a pack of wolves
Angry bear at their hooves.
Ivan thought he was going to die
Him and bear locked eye to eye.

The bear gave a growl,
The wolves ran off with a howl
The bear got down on all four feet
To be saved was a real treat.

Ivan entered Starjik's cave
Ivan was really brave
Ivan threw the ears in Starjik's face
And said:
'Brothers never more shall part,
Melt the winter in his heart.'

The tears melted Starjik's heart,
Ivan and his brother never would be apart
Starjik gave the children soup
They all felt like an ice cream scoop.

Curtis Shiers (9)
Millbrook Junior School

The Ice Palace

Ivan lived by Pine Wood Forest,
Where they had a good florist,
Winter is Starjik's feast,
When he travels to the east,
Brothers never more shall part,
Melt the winter in his heart.

Ivan knew wolves were by,
He climbed a tree really high,
An old woman gave him tears,
And these are the words Ivan hears,
'Brothers never more shall part,
Melt the winter in his heart.'

Ivan entered the dark cave,
He saw a man with a wrinkly age,
There was his brother,
It was like they looked at one another,
Brothers never more shall part,
Melt the winter in his heart.

Ivan flung the tears,
In Starjik's face,
With fear from head to toe,
Starjik laughed in no fright,
Brothers never more shall part,
Melt the winter in his heart.

All the ice began to melt,
Ivan began to feel,
His brother at his heel,
Starjik gave them soup and fur,
Brothers never more shall part,
There is no winter in his heart.

Amy Davies (9)
Millbrook Junior School

The Ice Palace

Ivan lives to the east
Where there is a kidnapping beast
The summer is short
The winter is long
All the children are nearly gone
Brothers never be alone
Ivan will find him on his own

All the wolves want me for supper
But Ivan needs a nice cuppa
The wind is blowing in my ears
And it's giving Ivan many more fears
Brothers never be alone
Ivan will find him on his own

Ivan loves his brother deep down
Ivan will find him, take him home
He won't be alone
Ivan will throw the tears in his eyes
Watch him change, he will be nice
Brothers never be alone
Ivan will take him home

Every winter Starjik's nice
He doesn't trap people behind that ice
Every day he will play
They will sing a song all day
Brothers never be alone
Ivan will take him home.

Ben Simms (10)
Millbrook Junior School

Stories Down Under

Under the blue, shimmering sea
Lies thousands of swiftly swaying reefs,
Seaweed flowing calmly,
Suddenly silence breaks,
Waves with violent tempers,
Sharks wailing through water creating riots,
Down under appears a whirlpool,
Reefs swaying but not swiftly,
Bodies falling in water drowning,
Reunited with old friends at the bottom of the sea,
Storm's over,
Back to normal.

Forgotten pirates drowning, sinking to the seabed,
Underneath in the shipwrecks,
Treasure lay, not touched,
Hidden in boundaries of sea caves,
New stories to remember,
That lost ship, those lost pirates.

Samantha Jo Elliott (11)
Millbrook Junior School

The Shipwreck

Under the gloomy, shimmering ocean,
Lies a gloomy, broken, rusty shipwreck,
Seaweed swaying in the water,
Broken anchors lying still on the seabed,
Forgotten treasure and ships fading away.
Underneath the wavy water lie ancestors of people,
Treasure still shining in the deep, deep ocean,
Stories of pirates still being told.

Ashley Bastow (11)
Millbrook Junior School

My Firework Poem

Fireworks bang
Fireworks roar
Fireworks are noisy
Fireworks swish
Fireworks are curly
Fireworks fizz
Fireworks zoom
Fireworks are colourful
Fireworks are *dangerous!*

Fireworks are red
Fireworks are yellow
Fireworks are orange
Fireworks are pink
Fireworks are green
Fireworks are blue
Fireworks are purple
Fireworks are silver
Fireworks are gold.

Alana Dalton-Francis (7)
Millbrook Junior School

Dog

Cat chaser
Rabbit racer
Belly scratcher
Ball catcher
Food eater
Human beater
Worm killer
Child partner
Food snatcher
Dog lover.

Bradley Satchell (10)
Millbrook Junior School

Dog

Tail wagger
Cat slapper
Biscuit cruncher
Food muncher
Day dreamer
Fur cleaner
Water drinker
Eye blinker
Car chaser
Dog racer
Ankle biter
Postman fighter
Flea scratcher
Ball catcher
Dogs forever
Always together.

Chelsie Cadman (11)
Millbrook Junior School

Dolphin

Big flipper
Fast swimmer
Water ripper
Wave jumper
Fish catcher
People lover
Piggyback giver
Fish breather
Dolphin lover.

Joanne Morgan (10)
Millbrook Junior School

The Magicians

They lived here
Thousands of years ago
And could do anything
They could save the village from a savage beast
Or maybe they could give the poor a massive feast
They could make the poor rich
And save the world from an evil witch
They could heal the wounded with a single touch
They could do any powerful spell as such
They could teleport anywhere with a puff of smoke
They could change their enemies into old folk.

Kai Jones (11)
Millbrook Junior School

Under The Sea

Under the sea an old, rusty ship
Lies in the shimmering deep blue,
Seaweed glittering from the sunlight,
Broken ships still have treasure floating around.

Forgotten treasures lie
Underneath the sea
Treasure like diamonds out of stories
From the past.

Joshua Skillern (10)
Millbrook Junior School

Daisy

There was a girl called Daisy
Who was so very lazy,
She stayed in bed
And rested her head
Until the sun was hazy.

Conor Gough (11)
Millbrook Junior School

Falling

Falling,
Falling,
Falling,
Down, deeper into the dark ocean.

Seashells swirling around me,
I fall into mountains of coral and slimy seaweed,
Memories of my loved ones swirl around me,
Charlie swimming through holes in shipwrecks
Vicious, hungry sharks snapping around me,
Schools of fish swimming in front of me.
My memories are
Gone,
Gone,
Gone.

Brogan Keepin (11)
Millbrook Junior School

Seashore Book

Open up this seashore book,
It's so special, take a look.
And don't forget to search for treasure,
Keep your eyes both open wide.
There's lots of things to be discovered,
Washed up by the morning tide.

Sarah Archer (10)
Millbrook Junior School

Sun Haiku

Shining in the sky
Counting all his gold treasure
Smiling gleefully.

Gemma Bates (10)
Millbrook Junior School

Full Fathom Five I Fall

Falling,
Falling,
Falling,
Full fathom five I fall
Deeper and deeper into the dark ocean,
Seashells slowly scattering to the bottom of the seabed.
Sea nymphs protecting their secret treasure.
Sharks feasting on the flesh of pirates.
Eels squirming through bones of dead people.
Giant clams protecting their giant pearls.
Sharks roaring around the wrecks of rotting ships.
Reaching the bottom I feel myself . . .
Going,
Going,
Going.

Rhys Coulson (11)
Millbrook Junior School

The Storm

The storm is a bully,
Ought to be sorted out;
He beats up the trees,
Then finishes them off
By throwing lightning at them,
Or roaring at them with thunder.
The storm is a bully,
Thrashing birds' nests out of bushes
And frightening everyone away.
He ought to be sorted out,
Needs to be bullied himself,
Getting a taste of his own medicine!

Emily Ann Merry (11)
Millbrook Junior School

Evil

Evil is spooky and scary
He thinks he is tough but he is rough.
He'll get you a rabbit then go and grab it
He's very mean, he is so keen.
He is the greatest of them all
If you stare at his hair you will be mesmerised
And if you stare at his beady eyes
You will be bitten on the arm.
At nightfall his eyes glow up.

Jordanne Leigh Setterfield (8)
Millbrook Junior School

Treasure Under The Sea

Under the sparkling sea,
Lies mouldy old, green bones.
Treasure shimmers in the distance,
And stories of adventure and rum.

Forgotten for years,
Underneath the sea.
Seaweed, rotten, brown and green,
Broken hearts deep down, deep down as can be.

Holly Goldsworthy (11)
Millbrook Junior School

Under The Deep, Blue Sea

Under the deep blue sea
Lies a snapped old boat with seaweed around it
Swishing and swaying
Broken skulls with rusted anchors
And bones under the deep blue sea
Forgotten people in shipwrecks
Underneath the broken bones is the treasure chest
Treasure with gems, diamonds, gold and silver.

Ben Fisher (11)
Millbrook Junior School

Snakes

Snake shaker
Snake breaker
Venom killer
Round hunter
Loud hisser
King slitherer
Tree crawler
Fowl eater
Big beater
Pedal swimmer
Jumping bumper
Shed ripper
Massive hitter
Proud sander.

Joshua Edwards (11)
Millbrook Junior School

The Evil Sun

The sun is an evil king,
Circles the world all day,
Scorching the slugs and snails
With its evil beams,
No one dares to look
Or a slash of his sword
Will cross your neck.

The sun is fighting for the world,
His velvet cloak blue with white fur,
Burning all his enemies,
Drying up all the water.

Ryan Smith (11)
Millbrook Junior School

Cats

Tail flicker
Mouse catcher
Night hunter
Milk licker
Ball taker
Fire scrammer
Kitten carrier
Wet hater
Moon lover
Claw scrambler
Cat lover
Cats forever.

Rebecca Jade Duke (10)
Millbrook Junior School

Best Friend

Shona's my best friend
Without her I feel like
A bird without wings,
A pedal-less bike,
A door with no hinge,
A star with no shine,
A book with no lines,
A head with no brain,
A storm with no rain,
A train with no steam,
A window with no gleam.

Billie Lee Palmer (10)
Millbrook Junior School

Queen Nefertiti

Spin a top, spin a bottle
All go up
Queen Nefertiti
Stalks through the day.

Over the skyscraper
Her feet go numb
Her legs are as cold
As a polar bear.

Her fingers are ice
Like an icicle
In the air
The mountain cracks
Open at her black-eyed stare.

Her voice is low
As a bear's low moan
She will steal your soul
She will make your body freeze.

Spin a bottle, spin a top
All go up
Queen Nefertiti
Stalks through the day.

Jacob Richards (9)
Millbrook Junior School

Shark

Meat eater
Fish chaser
Skin slicer
People scarer
People chewer
Evil hunter
Fish murderer
Death bringer.

Morgan Lingard & Kyle Vodden (10)
Millbrook Junior School

Ice Palace

Ivan lived in the distant east
Where children became a winter feast
Starjik wasn't very nice
He turned little children into ice

Ivan met lots of people
Later he found out it was Starjik's evil
He found himself in front of a hole
If ho'd danced any more he would be frozen cold
Brothers never more shall part
Melt the winter in his heart

Ivan carried on with his quest
He had no time to sleep and rest
He heard a sound like a jackal
There was an old woman
Who gave him tears
To make him forget his fears
Brothers never more shall part
Melt the winter in his heart

Ivan saw a glistening cave
Then he thought, *this is my grave*
He grabbed the tears
And forgot his fears
Flinging the tears he said,
'Brothers never more shall part,
Melt the winter in his heart.'

Then Starjik let the children go
They happily ran home in the snow
Brothers never more shall part
There is no winter in Starjik's heart.

Kristoffer Maybry (9)
Millbrook Junior School

Ice Palace

Ivan lived in the distant east,
Where children became a winter feast,
Starjik was an evil beast,
He killed the bats to make a feast.
Ivan crept out of his house one night,
He knew he would give his mother a fright.
Brothers never more shall part,
Melt the winter in his heart.

On the way to Starjik's land,
He built a snowdrift to keep him alive.
Up above in the sky he saw a snowy owl passing by,
He saw an old lady who gave him some tears.
'You will need these for your great fears.
Brothers never more shall part,
Melt the winter in his heart.'

When he arrived in Starjik's cave,
He thought his brother would never be saved.
Brothers never more shall part,
Melt the winter in his heart.

He threw the tears in Starjik's face,
'Brothers never more shall part,
Melt the winter in his heart.'

The children were so happy to be free
Starjik gave them soup as a treat.
His mother was happy to see them.
Brothers never more shall part,
The winter has gone in Starjik's heart.

Alicia Redman (10)
Millbrook Junior School

The Ice Palace

Ivan lived in the distant east
Where children were a winter feast
Ivan's brother was ripped from his bed
Starjik's been but now he's fled
Brothers never more shall part
Melt the winter in his heart

On the way to Starjik's land
Ivan saw wolves out of hand
They chased and snapped at Ivan's heels
Ivan leapt into the pine needles
Brothers never more shall part
Melt the winter in his heart

The bear was coming through the snow
He scared the pack away
The bear seemed to save Ivan that day
Ivan met a magical lady
Who gave him some frozen tears
She said, 'Use these tears
And throw them at Starjik's face
Brothers never more shall part
Melt the winter in his heart.'

Throwing the tears at Starjik's face
Ivan said, 'You're just a disgrace.'
Now the children are free at last
Starjik's gone and he's not coming back
Brothers never more shall part
Melt the winter in Starjik's heart.

Louis Hillberg & Jack Watkins (10)
Millbrook Junior School

Ice Palace

Ivan lived in the distant east
Where children became a winter feast
Starjik was nasty and cruel
He thought everyone was a fool
Brothers never more shall part
Melt the winter in Starjik's heart

Ivan was on a dangerous quest
Starjik was putting Ivan to the test
Ivan wrapped his coat tight
Protection for the freezing night

An old woman held out her hand
She said, 'You must go to Starjik's land,
Open this magical, glittering case
Throw the frozen tears at Starjik's face and say
Brothers never more shall part
Melt the winter in Starjik's heart.'

Ivan went into Starjik's cave of ice
He found out it was a palace of evil
Starjik was sitting on his frozen chair
He had evil, dirty, straggly hair.

Ivan threw the tears at Starjik's face
Then he became really ace
All the children were happy and free
When they passed the forest trees
Brothers never more shall part
Ivan melted the winter in Starjik's heart.

Chloe Smith (9)
Millbrook Junior School

The Night Leaf

First there were two of us then three of us
Then there was one leaf more
We floated down to the bumpy ground
Staring at the cotton candy clouds above
Suddenly an almighty snatch whisked us away
Twirling, twirling around all day

A shadow appeared casting darkness on all the world
Swirling droplets of light could be seen twinkling in the sky
I passed over mountains of ice cream
Hearing howling *a-tu-whit tu-whoo!*

I danced in the night without fright
Suddenly the sun rises, another day full of surprises.
My journey from my tree has finally come to an end
Now I will turn around my last bend
Laying on the carpeted floor with leaves that have fallen before.

Alice Kate Pritchard (10)
Millbrook Junior School

Autumn Leaves

First there was one of us then there were three of us
Then there was one leaf more
We floated down and lay on the floor
Waiting for someone to rake us up
But nobody cared about us
They stamped, chucked and trod on us
They thought we were dead
No one seemed to care for us sleeping in our leafy bed
Except one lady who took us in her warm house
And placed us with the other leaves
To make a pretty autumn frieze.

Michael Moynihan (10)
Millbrook Junior School

At My School

At my school I hear the twiggy trees
Bristling as the wind goes by.
I hear greasy chips sizzling in the canteen.
I hear the zooming cars whiz by.

I see mathematical children working.
I see the smartly-dressed Head walking around.
I see wild children running madly around the playground.

I feel overjoyed when I go to maths class
And I touch the shimmering paper.
I feel upset if I fall in the playground.

As I run round the playground
In the fresh, clear air,
I smell the bubbling cabbage
From the canteen.

My school rocks!

Morgan Elliott (8)
Penyrheol Primary School

At My School

At my school I see,
Horrendous clouds outside my see-through window.
Every day I see my friendly friends smiling.
I see my teacher's glasses because she loses them every day.
I feel the inky, runny pen I use to write on my paper.
I feel creased, white paper.
I feel the chair I love to sit on.
I hear teachers babbling and chatting all the time.
I hear my squeaky, flat, broken pen that has worn out.
I hear the caretaker hammering in nails and repairing lots of
                                        damaged things.
I smell tomatoes bursting with bitter red juice in the canteen,
At my school.

Ellie Evans (7)
Penyrheol Primary School

At My School

At my school I hear swishing trees
When all is silent.
I hear the rain tipping down on my class window.
I hear slamming metal gates.

I smell fresh oranges and apples at playtime.
I smell the chocolate chip cookies.
I smell minty paint when I paint.

I taste the fresh fish and chips
And a dollop of ketchup.
I taste the fruit - but never like them.

I see children playing chase.
I see the caretaker rushing down the corridor.
I see my exhausted teachers marking books.

I touch the watery, inky pens,
And the solid clay as I make a jewellery pot.
I touch my problem solving sheet which is everlasting.

I feel joy as I pick up an interesting book.
I feel hungry as I queue for dinner.
I feel excited as my sandwich box is put in front of me.

My school is the best school in the whole universe.

Amy Gibbons (8)
Penyrheol Primary School

My School

I hear the icy wind tapping at the crystal clear windows,
As if it is trying to enter the noisy classroom.
I see the sparkling emerald-green grass in the flowing fields
From where I sit.
I feel nervous when I am called to the nerve-wracking blackboard.
I smell the wonderful wafts of dinner
And taste the mouth-watering, freshly cooked dinners at lunchtime.

My school is spectacular.

Nicholas Powell (8)
Penyrheol Primary School

My School

At my school I hear strict teachers shouting.
I hear the clock ticking loudly during lessons.
I hear the zipping of people's coats in the morning.
I hear the board rubber sliding across the dark board.

I look at the trees through the transparent windows.
I see children working hard at their desks.
I see children playing in the playground.

I smell the freshly baked food,
And I smell feet when we go to PE.
I smell the breeze through the open window.

I feel joy when we do maths, history and science.
I feel proud when I do my work beautifully.
I feel joyful when I go home and tell my parents
What we have been doing.

My school is fantastic.

Emelia Russell (9)
Penyrheol Primary School

My School

I hear the young children
Slurping up water in the classrooms nervously.
I see the hardworking pupils studying maths.
I feel happy when the noisy buzzer goes for playtime
Because I know I can play with my friends.
I smell the greasy food from the canteen,
And I touch the wrinkly hands of my teacher
As she greets me into school.

My school is spotless.

Zoe Belton (8)
Penyrheol Primary School

My School

I hear cheeky children,
I hear pens writing,
And trays rattling.

I see concentrating children,
Teachers helping children,
Happy children writing.

I feel the table wriggling,
A book being written on,
And paperclips being fixed on a piece of paper.

I smell soapy hands,
White chalk,
And shampoo on people's hair.

I know my school is the best school in the whole wide world.

Victoria Robinson (7)
Penyrheol Primary School

My School

I hear the bellowing teachers exploding
As children continue to misbehave.

I see the midnight dark, blackboard staring at me.
I see hyperactive children messing about in the classroom.

I feel warm inside with a hard pumping inside me
As I face the teacher.

I taste sizzling food in the canteen,
The bubbling cabbage, and the burning sausages.

My school is super.

Sophie Davies (8)
Penyrheol Primary School

My School

At my school I hear the rushing cars go by.
I hear the bluebirds singing joyfully in their nests.
I hear the teachers bellowing at children,
And the children mumbling.

I see children chanting.
I see boys in the playground playing football.
I see children interested in their stories.

I smell the dusty chalk that makes me sneeze.
I smell healthy food in the air,
And the fresh breeze.

I feel the rock hard table,
Where I write.
I feel joy as soon as I walk through the school doors.

My school is beautiful.

Courtney Evans (9)
Penyrheol Primary School

My School

At my school I hear naughty children
Talking during lessons.
I hear children fussing,
And others being funny.

I felt embarrassed on my first day at school.
I feel embarrassed when I call my teacher 'Mum'.
I get cross when I am called names.

I smell perfume on the girls.
I smell sweat when we play dodgeball in the hall.

I love the feel of inky pens.
I feel happiness when I go through the classroom doors.
And I feel happy when it's home time!

My school is wicked.

Curtis Hovvels (7)
Penyrheol Primary School

At My School

At my school I hear the sound of
Clicking on the computer.
I can hear children working
And birds whistling in the trees.

I see children playing in the playground
And speedy cars going past.
I see Miss doing work
And children making tores.

I smell beautiful flowers in the flower pot.
I smell the fresh curry from the kitchen.

I feel happy when we go on trips,
Happy when we do paintings.
I feel happy when we play on the computer.

And my school is cool.

Sam Woods (9)
Penyrheol Primary School

My School

At my school I see chatting, fussing children.
I see the roaring teacher.
I see the cook giving out delicious foods.

I touch the greasy plates in the canteen,
And I feel the smooth Blu-tack on the display board.

I hear the tweeting songbirds,
And listen to the wonderful, quiet class,
And the lovely children reading.

I love my school.

Anya Russell (8)
Penyrheol Primary School

At My School

As I sit working
I hear the zooming cars on the road.
As I play in the yard
I see the singing birds in their nests.
When I am writing
I feel the flowing ink pens on my hands.
I touch the squeaky tray
When I am working in class.
I taste the gravel when I fall on the floor
Over the skipping rope in the playground,
And I try not to cry.

My school is cool.

Zak Fisher (8)
Penyrheol Primary School

My School

At my school I see
Working children with frowning faces,
And reading children.

I touch my glorious books,
My shiny pen,
And my special rubber.

I hear ranting teachers,
And talking children,
And I hear the peeling of
Award stickers.

I feel happy at school.

Gethin Sullivan (7)
Penyrheol Primary School

My School

At my school I hear the caretaker
Clattering around with his tools.
I hear the dinner ladies rushing about.
I can hear the teachers teaching.

I smell the disgusting cabbage
From the canteen,
And wonderful smells like fish and chips,
And astonishing perfume smells

I see the excitable children on the yard.
I see teachers helping other children.
I see children having fun as they work.

My school is exciting.

Alexander Murphy (7)
Penyrheol Primary School

My School

In my school I hear the breezy wind
Rustling in the trees during lessons.
I see the baby birds in their prickly nests.
I see the enjoyment of squirrels
Scuttling during class.
I feel happiness and joy
As I walk into class.
I taste the greasy pizzas
In my mouth at lunchtime,
And the mouth-watering dessert.

My school is the best in the world.

Lee Jones (8)
Penyrheol Primary School

My School

At my school I hear teachers roaring
And children chattering till they pop.
I see children with sapphire blue pens
And teacher bossing about with chalk.
I feel the warm, bumpy radiator
Warming up the tall, smooth wall.
I smell the wafting perfume
Drifting through the classroom,
Delicious food smells,
And freshly glued glue starting to dry in books.

But my school
Is absolutely fabulous.

Liam Matthews (9)
Penyrheol Primary School

My School

I hear loud, chattering children in their lessons.
I see the healthy boys and girls
Eating all their dinner in the school hall.

I feel joyful when the teachers say
We can go out into the playground.

I taste the lovely dinner in the canteen.
I touch the lovely, colourful walls.

Our school is superb.

Samuel Matthews (8)
Penyrheol Primary School

Happiness

Happiness is a variety of colours.
It sounds like happy, laughing people.
It tastes like happy, juicy love.
It smells like happy people.
It looks like happiness.
It reminds me of happy, smiling people.

Ellie Donohoe (7)
St Joseph's Cathedral Juniors, Swansea

Love

Love is red.
It sounds like a mother's tears dripping from her saddest eyes.
It tastes like a juicy jar of jam.
It smells like salt sea.
It looks like a gleaming smile.
It reminds me of my mother's love.

Ellie May Diamond (7)
St Joseph's Cathedral Juniors, Swansea

Emotions, Love

Love looks like a swarm of bees making lots of honey
Love tastes like a big chocolate sundae that never ends
Love sounds like angels singing in Heaven
Love feels like getting married
Love smells like a rare perfume.

Jordan Baker (8)
St Joseph's Cathedral Juniors, Swansea

The Haunted House

In the cellar is
    A cupboard with rats inside
    A black cat trying to get out of the window
    A mirror that gives no reflection
    A snake crawling through the door
And the only sound is
    A black cat scratching a window.

In the living room is
    A TV smashed in half
    A curtain which is ripped
    A sofa cut in half
    A picture of a skeleton
And the only sound is
    A heavy door creaking.

In the bedroom is
    An old doll talking
    A bed turned upside down
    A floor with no carpet
    A smashed window
And the only sound is
    The wind blowing.

In the attic is
    A piano being played by itself
    A toy bat squeaking in a corner
    A door being blown back and forth by the wind
    A jar full of beady eyes
And the only sound is
    The piano playing a tune.

Ryan Argyle (9)
St Joseph's Cathedral Juniors, Swansea

The Haunted House

In the kitchen is
    A coffin with a skeleton in it
    A rusty old wash machine
    A table and chairs wobbling
    A pair of white gloves making a cup of tea
And the only sound is
    Footsteps coming closer to me.

In the lounge is
    A rusty old sofa
    An old lamp floating around the room
    A TV playing by itself
    An old rocking chair
And the only sound is
    The rocking chair creaking.

In the bedroom is
    A bed with holes
    A jar with bones floating
    A bag of rats trying to get out
    A black chest waiting to be opened
And the only sound is
    The key to the chest clicking.

In the attic is
    A skeleton hanging from the ceiling
    A piano being played by itself
    A rusty bike
    A dead body lying on the floor
And the only sound is
    A door slamming.

Emily Draper (8)
St Joseph's Cathedral Juniors, Swansea

A Day In The Life Of Danny The Cat

Danny wakes up
Eats
Plays with his ball
Chases the mice
Runs away from a dog
And sleeps

Danny wakes up
Eats
Licks himself
Chases a piece of string
Mews
And sleeps

Danny wakes up
Eats
Fights another cat
Falls in love
Goes into the garage
And sleeps.

Joshua Nedin (8)
St Joseph's Cathedral Juniors, Swansea

Ryan's Pets

Ten tiny tarantulas tiptoeing to their prey
Nine nasty nits knitting all away
Eight wiggly earwigs licking one's ear
Seven hissing snakes, don't come too near
Six crawly spiders climbing up the wall
Five fluttering fireflies glowing like a ball
Four green frogs jumping up and down
Three small tadpoles trying not to drown
Two hard shell tortoises shine their shells anew
One large octopus waves goodbye to you.

Ryan Dark (8)
St Joseph's Cathedral Juniors, Swansea

The Haunted House

In the attic is
    A skeleton in a coffin overrun with mice
    A big cauldron full of curses
    A large white sheet floating
    A piano playing all by itself
And the only sound is
    The coffin opening with a creak.

In the lounge is
    A rocking chair moving itself
    A bike with only arms riding it
    A jar with ten beady eyes
    A headless monster
And the only sound is
    A door creaking.

In the cellar is
    A wall with creeping ivy
    A secret passageway
    A black cat by an old chest
    The chest being opened by rats
And the only sound is
    A chest opening with a click.

Lauren Ward (8)
St Joseph's Cathedral Juniors, Swansea

Ten Things In A Wizard's Pocket

A sword that extends to any length
A wand that shines when something is wrong
A plant that grows as high as you can imagine
A star that changes colour
Gold that drives enemies away
A bat that has teeth 1000cm long
A wooden toy that comes to life
A black cat
A scarf that moves
A clock that takes ten hours to get round.

Sougri Abugre (8)
St Joseph's Cathedral Juniors, Swansea

Robin's Pets

In his bedroom he kept
Ten tiny tarantulas tangling a web
Nine naughty newts nibbling a plant
Eight egg-laying eagles eating a mouse in the wardrobe
Seven slithering snakes sucking a lolly
Six sobbing seals swimming in a water tank
Five fluttering flamingos flying around the room
Four forest deer fighting on the bed
Three trotting tigers talking to their cubs
Two talking Tasmanian devils treating children like babies
One overweight octopus swimming with the seals.

Robin Bermudez (9)
St Joseph's Cathedral Juniors, Swansea

Love

Love is red
It sounds like a harp playing
It tastes like creamy chocolates
It smells like loving cherries
It looks like dreams in your head
It reminds me of an angel.

Emily Cooney (8)
St Joseph's Cathedral Juniors, Swansea

Love

Love is red
It sounds like a choir of angels
It tastes like juicy strawberries
It smells like roses
It looks like Cupid's arrow.

Kirra Williams (8)
St Joseph's Cathedral Juniors, Swansea

Mrs Jones' Pets

In her bedroom she kept
Ten tiny tigers scratching their claws
Nine naughty newts nibbling their tea
Eight enchanting emus tiptoeing around
Seven silly spiders spinning a web
Six sleepy snakes slithering around the room
Five fearless fowls frolicking about
Four friendly fawns sleeping on the bed
Three timid tortoises hiding under the bed
Two tiptoeing turtles eating the carpet
One - guess what?

Sophie Lloyd (8)
St Joseph's Cathedral Juniors, Swansea

Anger

Anger is dark red
It sounds like screeching fireworks
It tastes like steam
It smells like dragon's breath
It looks like a ruby-red bear
It reminds me of starting to cry.

Atlanta Martone (8)
St Joseph's Cathedral Juniors, Swansea

Happiness

Happiness is different colours
It sounds like children's laughter
It tastes like sweet sweets
It smells like a juicy strawberry
It looks like playful friends
It reminds me of playful people.

Georgia Davies (7)
St Joseph's Cathedral Juniors, Swansea

Wizards

In the wizard's pocket there was
A sign that was invisible,
A green and red singing frog,
A purse of magic money,
A hanky that was the size of a rubber,
A beautiful golden goose that lays silver eggs,
A book that never ends,
A pen made of ice,
A knight in a fairy costume,
A spider the size of a castle,
A pair of creepy hands.

Alicia McCabe (9)
St Joseph's Cathedral Juniors, Swansea

Likes And Dislikes

What I hate about babies is they scream most of the time.
What I like about babies is they are really, really cute.

What I hate about cats is they dig their claws in your legs.
What I like about cats is they warm up your lap.

What I hate about painting is you get paint on your hands.
What I like about painting is it is really fun.

Katie Davis (7)
St Joseph's Cathedral Juniors, Swansea

Emotions

Excited is when you have to boast
Looks like your favourite toy
Tastes like a Sunday lunch
Sounds like music playing quietly from the west
Feels like a surprise present
Smells like a flower in the air
Excited is when you have to boast.

Lucy Jenkins (8)
St Joseph's Cathedral Juniors, Swansea

A Friend

A lways kind.

F riendship lasts forever.
R emembers you when you're sad.
I enjoy a happy playtime.
E ven though I am sad my friends cheer me up.
N ever shout at me.
D on't fight.

Luke Cardone (8)
St Joseph's Cathedral Juniors, Swansea

Through The Door

I am inside looking outside
At the dogs barking
I am outside looking inside
At my mother sleeping

I am inside looking outside
At the cats fighting
I am outside looking inside
At some people eating.

Joel Wayne Morris (8)
St Joseph's Cathedral Juniors, Swansea

Anger

Anger is when your head turns to red-hot fire,
Anger looks like a tsunami of goo,
Anger sounds like an angry mob,
Anger feels like 1000 swords sticking into you,
Anger smells like a tonne of garbage,
Anger is when your temperature rises beyond control.

Callum Daniel (9)
St Joseph's Cathedral Juniors, Swansea

Ryan's Pets

In his bedroom Ryan kept
Ten ants that crawled and scurried up the walls,
Nine frogs that hopped and jumped on the leaves,
Eight birds that sung up in the trees and flew on the house,
Seven mice that ran around Ryan's bedroom
And jumped up on his bed,
Six cats that scraped the wallpaper and ran after the mice,
Five wolves that were black and brown, howled in the night,
Four different coloured cheetahs
That ran very fast around the room,
Three hippos that were grey,
Two elephants drinking Ryan's juice and making loud noises,
One, guess what? . . . A giraffe eating all the plants in the garden.

Rhys Jones (8)
St Joseph's Cathedral Juniors, Swansea

Lauren's Pets

In her bedroom Lauren kept
Ten horses that galloped around the room
Nine spiders that walked up everything
Eight hamsters that jumped around the cage
Seven crazy dogs that barked at the light bulb
Six big and lazy pigs
Five cats after the mice
Four mice, pink and blue and little
Three big snakes slithering on the ground
Two stripy zebras trotting around the room
One little monster who is with them.

Lauren Baskerville (8)
St Joseph's Cathedral Juniors, Swansea

Chloe's Pets

In her bedroom she kept
Ten tiny tarantulas hanging from the door
Nine noisy newts hiding in the bed
Eight eating eagles nibbling gone-off eggs
Seven slimy snakes hiding under the blankets
Six slippery sea lions in the wardrobe
Five frightened falcons pecking at the door
Four fluffy flamingos perched by the window
Three tidy tigers hiding behind the wardrobe
Two terrifying Tasmanian wolves guarding the door
Only one octopus lying on the bed.

Chloe Hayden (9)
St Joseph's Cathedral Juniors, Swansea

John's Pets

Ten tiny tadpoles swimming in a tank
Nine naughty newts nibbling the carpet
Eight eerie eels wriggling around
Seven slippery snakes slithering on the ground
Six skilful seals showing off their tricks
Five furry foxes chasing their tails
Four frisky foals playing outside
Three troublesome tigers with nowhere to hide
Two tiger sharks snapping their teeth
One giant octopus floating underneath.

John Collins (9)
St Joseph's Cathedral Juniors, Swansea

My Hamster

Ten runs on his wheel and sniffs
Nine sips from his bottle
Eight nibbles of hamster food
Seven jumps on his house
Six scratches every day
Five tunnels being dug up all the time
Four little steps every day
Three rolls over on my bed
Two googly eyes staring at me

One . . . little monster nibbling his cage.

Joseph Thomas (9)
St Joseph's Cathedral Juniors, Swansea

A Wizard's Pocket

A teacher in boiling lava
An upside down school
A castle made of flowers
A swarm of green elephants
An evil dad that gave no pocket money
A world full of fire
A very, very black stormy night
A bus with a demon teacher
A haunted cup you drink blood out of
A friendly ghost that gives you sweets.

Ben Lloyd (9)
St Joseph's Cathedral Juniors, Swansea

My Apple Poem

My apple is as red as a cherry.
It tastes like a berry.
It sounds like there is nothing there.
It feels like a rock.
My apple is like a flashing ball.

Anthony Loibl (9)
St Joseph's Cathedral Juniors, Swansea

It's My Room Not Theirs

In my room I have
Ten puppy dogs that bite, chew and crowd around
    It's my room not theirs
Nine annoying seals that balance balls and clubs
    It's my room not theirs
Eight enormous cats that chew, bite and scratch
    It's my room not theirs
Seven stupid sloths, there I am using dusters and cloths
I do my very best but they still make a mess
    It's my room not theirs
Six slimy snails slide and slither around the room
    It's my room not theirs
Five fat frogs croaking everywhere
They treat the room as their own
There are animals to and fro
    It's my room not theirs
Four monkeys that swing
They just decided to move in
    It's my room not theirs
Three scuttling spiders weaving loads of webs
I mean, just look at my poor bed
    It's my room not theirs
Two tiny rabbits sprinting like hares
They're alright but then there's
One of me clearing it all up
I'm really just too tired
And I just give up!

Sarah Passmore (8)
St Joseph's Cathedral Juniors, Swansea

Summer Haiku

On a bright morning
I wake up to a fun day
And go to the beach.

Scott Hopkins (8)
St Joseph's Cathedral Juniors, Swansea

A Day In The Life Of Danny The Cat

Danny wakes up
Eats
Plays
Jumps
Goes to next door
And sleeps

Danny wakes up
Eats
Chases a mouse
Plays with some plants
Looks for a lovely place in the garden
And sleeps.

Jordan Bevan (8)
St Joseph's Cathedral Juniors, Swansea

Love

Love is red
It sounds like raindrops
It tastes like strawberry jam
It smells like perfume
It looks like the sun rising
It reminds me of a smile.

Connah Troy (8)
St Joseph's Cathedral Juniors, Swansea

Love

Love is red.
Love sounds like rain in autumn.
Love tastes like romantic things.
Love smells like Jesus.
Love looks like a little drop of water.
Love reminds me of Jesus.

Chelsea Jones (7)
St Joseph's Cathedral Juniors, Swansea

Sean's Pets

In his bedroom he kept
Ten tiny tarantulas tiptoeing through a web
Nine naughty newts nibbling Nan's nose
Eight energetic eagles eating eyes
Seven snakes squabbling over scented soap
Six baby sharks sitting snugly on a stone
Five feathery flamingos flying thoughtfully
Four furry foxes fighting for food
Three terrible tigers running through the en suite
Two terrifying tapirs tearing towels
One 'orrible ostrich opening oranges.

Sean McCabe (9)
St Joseph's Cathedral Juniors, Swansea

Love

Love is red
It sounds like true love
It tastes like raspberries
It smells like love perfume
It looks like blood dripping
It reminds me of love.

Keeanna Cullen (7)
St Joseph's Cathedral Juniors, Swansea

Love

Love is red roses
It sounds like a mother's lullaby
It tastes like juicy grapes
It smells like a shiny red rose
It looks like a heart of roses
It reminds me of Jesus.

Leah Palmer (7)
St Joseph's Cathedral Juniors, Swansea

Poetry Performance

Seven little children
Eating pic 'n' mix
A hole appeared and one fell out
And then there were six

Six little children
At a beehive
Out came a spider
And then there were five

Five little children
Playing on the floor
One went to the door
And then there were four

Four little children
Had a bad knee
One went for a wee
And then there were three

Three little children
Cuddling a child
The child went boo
And then there were two

Two little children
Kissing their mum
Along came their sister
And then there was one.

Lily Thomas (7)
St Joseph's Cathedral Juniors, Swansea

Love

Love is red, the colour of the sun
It sounds like birds flapping their wings
It tastes like the blowing wind
It looks like the flowers growing.

Samuel Reseigh (7)
St Joseph's Cathedral Juniors, Swansea

Poetry Performance

Seven little children
Playing with some sticks
Along came a dragon
And then there were six

Six little children
Went past a hive
Out came a bee
And then there were five

Five little children
Playing on the floor
Along came a dinosaur
And then there were four

Four little children
Going for a wee
One disappeared
And then there were three.

Dylan Driscoll (8) & Lorna Cozens (7)
St Joseph's Cathedral Juniors, Swansea

Poetry Performance

Seven little children
Building some bricks
One got stuck
And then there were six

Six little children
Throwing a beehive
One got stung
And then there were five

Five little children
Laughing at a boar
The boar got mad
And then there were four.

John Bermudez (8)
St Joseph's Cathedral Juniors, Swansea

Poetry Performance

Seven little children
Playing lots of tricks
One blew away
And then there were six

Six little children
Watching TV live
Along came a monster
And then there were five

Five little children
Breaking the law
Along came a policeman
And then there were four

Four little children
Waiting for me
Along came four bullies
And then there were three

Three little children
Playing with a shoe
Along came a lion
And then there were two.

Caitlin Dorrell-Hunt (7)
St Joseph's Cathedral Juniors, Swansea

Love

Love is red.
It sounds like a lullaby.
It tastes like milkshake.
It smells like gone-off perfume.
It looks like the river.
It reminds me of Jesus.

Kieran Parkhouse (8)
St Joseph's Cathedral Juniors, Swansea

Love

Love is red.
It sounds like the wind.
It tastes like red apples.
It smells like flying in the air.
It looks like a baby.
It reminds me of Jesus.

Jessica Davies (8)
St Joseph's Cathedral Juniors, Swansea

Happiness

Happiness is yellow.
It sounds like a drop of raindrops.
It tastes like mint ice cream.
It smells like juicy jelly.
It looks like sunshine.
It reminds me of gleaming smiles.

Jade Barry (7)
St Joseph's Cathedral Juniors, Swansea

Love

Love is red
It sounds like a heart pumping
It tastes like strawberry milkshake
It smells like strawberry perfume
It looks like a red heart
It reminds me of Jesus.

Nicole O'Connell (8)
St Joseph's Cathedral Juniors, Swansea

Ten Things Found In A Wizard's Pocket

A glowing cat
A hand that steals
A pen that writes on its own
A bag of wasps found in stars
A lion that thinks it's a mouse
A cup that refills
A ball that makes stars
A stool that shrinks.

Sophie Morgan-Key (8)
St Joseph's Cathedral Juniors, Swansea

Love

Love looks like an angel singing in the sky
Love makes me remember my mother crying
It smells like gorgeous perfume
It tastes like chocolate cake
It sounds like water drops
Falling down on the windows.

Jake Hoskin (8)
St Joseph's Cathedral Juniors, Swansea

Anger

Anger is black
Anger is nasty
Anger smells like onions
It tastes like rotten eggs.

Daniel Duggins (7)
St Joseph's Cathedral Juniors, Swansea

John's Pets

In his bedroom John kept
Ten earwigs crawling all over the room
Nine butterflies that fluttered around
Eight hamsters that were scampering in the cage
Seven goldfish that swam around the fishbowl
Six cats being chased by the dogs
Five dogs chasing the six cats
Four eagles flying across the room
Three Siberian tigers chasing the dogs
Two lions chasing the tigers
And *one* . . . great white shark that ate the goldfish.

Anthony Barletta (8)
St Joseph's Cathedral Juniors, Swansea

The Magic Basket

In my magic basket there are:
Ten blue diamonds
Nine razor-sharp swords
Eight enormous stretch limos
Seven big mansions
Six monkey servants
Five tall bodyguards
Four red motorbikes
Three splatting paintball guns
Two flaming jet packs
One best friend.

Dyfri Schmidhamer (11)
St Monica's CW Primary School, Cardiff

Magic Basket

In my magic basket there are:
Ten rubies, wonderful and bright, shining in the sun.
Nine gold coins, enormous and gold in the bright light.
Eight big, beautiful lamps shining.
Seven nice kind friends always happy.
Six little diamonds, valuable and sparkly.
Five white pearls gleaming.
Four guns, black, popping.
Three maps with an X.
Two crystal balls, nice and big.
One crystal, fat and plump.

Michele Montersino (8)
St Monica's CW Primary School, Cardiff

The Magic Basket

In my magic basket there are
Ten naughty friends getting into mischief,
Nine fantastic fairies making magic,
Eight zooming cars ready to go,
Seven gorgeous models walking down the catwalk,
Six glittery jewels showing off,
Five lovely cats shining in the sun,
Four swimming swimmers faster than everyone,
Three dogs jumping round and round,
Two bees flying like butterflies,
One door to life.

Rimsha Ali (9)
St Monica's CW Primary School, Cardiff

The Magic Basket

In my magic basket there are:
Ten fireworks shooting like a shooting star.
Nine golden coins sparkling and shining
Like a disco ball shimmering.
Eight magical apple trees with ripe and juicy apples.
Seven pieces of jewellery so sparkly they could blind you.
Six magical lamps that can wish any wish.
Five friends playing together happily.
Four fishes swimming peacefully and quietly.
Three birds tweeting joyfully.
Two dolphins swimming joyfully.
One golden goose glittering and golden.

Gbenga Omirinde (10)
St Monica's CW Primary School, Cardiff

Magic Basket

In my magic basket there are:
Ten golden rings healing people.
Nine magic stars dashing through the sky.
Eight great friends playing with me all the time.
Seven fish swinging in the shiny water.
Six sunny books making me laugh.
Five lovely magic hats granting my wishes.
Four golden clouds sparkling with gold.
Three tiny planets next to the hot sun.
Two lovely classrooms full of children.
One huge boiling sun keeping us warm.

Sulli Richards (9)
St Monica's CW Primary School, Cardiff

Magic Basket

In my magic basket there are:
Ten glistening coins shimmering in the sun,
Nine green shining rubies lying in the sand,
Eight silverfish swimming through the deep blue sea
Seven generous friends whooshing through the air,
Six beautiful birds swooping up and down,
Five golden cats having a play,
Four postcards from America with a picture of Disney on the front,
Three packets of sweet wrappers shining like stars,
Two people dancing in the moonlight,
One gold lamp as shiny as the sun.

Joe Jones (8)
St Monica's CW Primary School, Cardiff

The Magic Basket

In my magic basket there are:
Ten scary pirate hats
Nine golden telescopes
Eight dark and evil pirate patches
Seven floating pirate ships
Six metal pirate belts
Five swaying palm trees
Four strong pirate crews
Three metal blazing swords
Two defence shields
One strong gun.

Ben Jones (10)
St Monica's CW Primary School, Cardiff

The Magic Basket

In my magic basket there are:
One glistening, shining sword,
And a flash of magic as soon as you open it,
You can see gold, silver and blue magic dust!
It has a gold, shimmering bird ornament,
12 gold coins, each one worth £100!
It has 15 silver diamonds and 5 rubies!
All sorts of gems, rubies, emeralds, sapphires and topaz!
In my magic basket there is
A swirl of red dust blasting everywhere around the basket
Just like a blast of fire
Zooming, blasting everywhere!

Danielle Nicole Paglionico (9)
St Monica's CW Primary School, Cardiff

Magic Basket

In my magic basket there are:
Ten golden coins sparkling lightly
Nine friends smiling nicely
Eight fireworks shooting in the sky fast
Seven fish swimming in the deep blue sea
Six apple trees with juicy apples
Five jet planes flying in the blue sky
Four genies granting wonderful wishes
Three cats sleeping on the blue sofa
Two pizzas grilling and popping
And one big statue of plain gold which heals the sick.

Jacob Fenner (9)
St Monica's CW Primary School, Cardiff

Magic Basket!

In my magic basket there is:
A world full of wonder where all your dreams come alive,
Take a look inside and you won't believe your eyes,
There is a:
Magical cat with a huge golden rat,
A big, glowing, yellow star and a special, sparkly waterfall
Flowing over a special car.
There is a glimmering angel that is flapping her glittery wings
And a ruby-red robin that actually sings.
There is a cute little fairy that is waiting to grant you a wish,
With her fat, scaly fish.
There is a glamorous, golden, ruby-red necklace
As golden as the sun
And a magic, bubbling mud pool as brown as a bun!
There is a blue topaz shining nicely at the bottom of the sea
And there is a big, big diamond floating happily with glee.

Sophie Lauren Bowen (10)
St Monica's CW Primary School, Cardiff

The Magic Basket

In my magic basket there are:
Ten shining sapphires reflecting the sun.
Nine glowing rubies glowing in the dark.
Eight naughty friends getting into mischief.
Seven speedy stars shooting in the sky.
Six wishing rainbow fish wishing every day.
Five gold coins shining in the sun.
Four special rings with diamonds falling out.
Three sparkling emeralds sparkling in the rain.
Two silver lions standing on a shelf.
One golden head, the God of all.

David Lee Flynn (10)
St Monica's CW Primary School, Cardiff

The Orchestra Of The Sea

The harmonic, heavenly harp
Played by a radiant mermaid sloshing in the midnight sea.
The clattering, clanging, clanking castanets of the daring dolphins
Calling their jam-packed school.
The constant moaning and droning
Of the draining didgeridoo speedboat engines.
The marvellous maracas make the noise
Of the courageous crabs' pinching claws.
The clashing waves
Crashing up against the wretched, rough rocks
Like golden cymbals.
The squawking screeching of the seagulls
As if they were a vigorous violin.
The bubbly, bouncing beach ball
Bobbing along the scorching sand to the beat of a drum.
Down below the depths of the ocean a scary shark
Is lurking in his evil layer,
He is the double bass.

Bethan Anne Watts (10)
St Monica's CW Primary School, Cardiff

The Magic Basket

In my magic basket there are:
Ten little stars dazzling like diamonds
Nine wishes dazzling like sapphires
Eight tiny fairies dazzling like opals
Seven dreams dazzling like butterflies
Six lights sparkling like stars
Five friends sparkling like gold
Four families sparkling like silver
Three unicorns sparkling like snow
Two angels sparkling like icicles
One god sparkling like magic.

Alice Wellock (8)
St Monica's CW Primary School, Cardiff

The Orchestra Of The Sea

Below the bottomless sea is the silent, stalking shark,
Moving to the tune of a triangle.
The mermaid sings softly,
Searching like a harsh harp.

The silver sea is sandy with the strong, wet, weaving waves
Like a xylophone.
A riot rises wreaking havoc,
This is the sound of an electric guitar.

The slippery, slimy seaweed screeches sorrowfully,
Like an out of control orchestra.
The children crunch on chips chewing them endlessly,
Sounding like the marvellous maracas.

David Rogers (10)
St Monica's CW Primary School, Cardiff

The Orchestra Of The Sea

The crashing, booming waves of the rough sea
Thrashing themselves into the solid rocks
Are tambourines being beaten by heavy, hard hands.

The high-pitched sound of happy children laughing
While running along the shore
Throwing a ball back and forth
Is a shaker shaking faster and faster.

The calm sound of the wind travelling so slowly
You could only feel its breeze.
The wind is a harp playing so softly
It will lift you away.

Megan Davies (10)
St Monica's CW Primary School, Cardiff

The Orchestra Of The Sea

As the day dawns the sea creatures rest,
Before the plague of the music thunder
Attacks those who are weak.
The people's childish chattering
Represents the exotic vibes of the castanets.
Happiness and laughter stain the salty sand
Imitating the unexpected guitar's tune.
Biting, chewing, munching and crunching.
The greasy, fatty food being quickly digested
By hungry pedestrians,
Slowly slurping their drinks as busy as maracas.

Everyone's enjoying the marvellous sight.
Suddenly the viewers leave and the musical plague commences,
A deadly storm breaks through into the scene.

Crashing waves, cliffs helplessly crumbling to the seabed,
All as quick and ear piercing
As the loudest cymbals you could find.
Although the night is still young,
The king of the sea still hasn't performed
For his fellow sea creatures.

The finale of this event ends
With all the bass instruments booming and banging together.
When it is all done the creatures rest once again;

For this is how the sea cycle works.

Pearl Mlambo (11)
St Monica's CW Primary School, Cardiff

The Orchestra Of The Sea

The deep blue sea is swirling calmly across the beach
Like the sound of a golden harp.
The big, round, fat bubbles float to the top of the sea
Like the popping sound of the drums.

Beneath the deep blue sea a shark awaits
Like the sound of a clock going tick-tock-tick-tock.
He hears the laughter of children like the sound of a xylophone,
He waits for something to drop.
Bang! Goes the drum.

Mohamed Binesmael (11)
St Monica's CW Primary School, Cardiff

The Orchestra Of The Sea

At the beach seagulls squawk like a piccolo
As they dip and soar above the sea.
During the night the wind and waves fight
To the sound of many drums.

The shark stalking for its food in the deep blue sea.
Children laughing as they play on the sand
Chattering and shouting like the percussion in an orchestra.

Tor Richards (11)
St Monica's CW Primary School, Cardiff

Magical Basket

In my magical basket there is:
A world full of beautiful, shimmering stars shining gold.
A huge pink pearl that appears to be
A beautiful, glistening flowers that shines in the dark night sky.
An emerald-green dragon that doesn't have flaming fire breath
But shiny snow breath that will put a smile on everybody's face.
A ruby-red, lovely rose which blows in the cool autumn breeze.
Soon the magic from the basket shall be revealed to all.

Fairooz Mostafa (10)
St Monica's CW Primary School, Cardiff

My Magic Box
(Based on 'Magic Box' by Kit Wright)

I will put in my box . . .
An exciting Christmas filled with joy,
The annoyance of the first time I saw my new house,
And the first time I saw a sand statue.

I will put in my box . . .
The first time I went on holiday,
The first time I saw my new school,
The memories I had with my dog.

I will put in my box . . .
A time when I was happy,
A time when I was sad,
A time when I looked scary at Hallowe'en.

My box is made from
Bright yellow petals shining in the light.
I shall close my box
And share it with the world.

Shorna Marie Buckley (9)
St Peter's RC Primary School, Cardiff

Fun

Fun is blue like a water park.
It smells like roses when they've just blossomed.
It feels like your teacher giving you a merit.
It looks like a big, secret waterfall.
It sounds like birds singing in the trees.
It tastes like a sweet and sour cherry drop.
It reminds me of trees swaying in the breeze.

Huw Thompson (10)
St Peter's RC Primary School, Cardiff

My Magic Box
(Based on 'Magic Box' by Kit Wright)

I will put in my box . . .
The freshest water from the ocean blue
A gold eagle from the snowy mountains
And fruit and plants from the rainforest.

I will put in my box . . .
People from all different cultures
The crispy pink bacon in the morning
An elk from the biggest forest
And a drop of the smoothest smoothie.

I will put in my box . . .
The shiniest star from the clear black sky
A blooming flower on the first day of summer
And an ice-cold ice cream on a hot day.

My box is fashioned from
Velvet silk cloth on each side with golden stars on top
The hinges are joined together with blue pearls
Hiding in the secret corners made from fish scales
And flower petals on the lid.

I shall hide my box
On a beach and put the map on the beach
For it to be dug up again.

Lauren Anne Byrne (9)
St Peter's RC Primary School, Cardiff

One Question From A Dagger

I want to give up being a dagger
I've been a dagger too long

I want to be a hobby horse
In the hand of a child
And be put up for show
In a clean, happy and loving home.

I want to give up being a dagger
I've been a dagger too long

I want to be a book
To be read by people
Providing rich information for generations
To smell fresh air
On a winter's day
Or to be a beautiful rose
In the fields unknown
With my ancestors.

I want to give up being a dagger
I've been a dagger for too long

The question is
Can you give up being a killer
And become free and happy?

Ryan Spriggs (10)
St Peter's RC Primary School, Cardiff

The Magic Box
(Based on 'Magic Box' by Kit Wright)

I will put in the box . . .
The kindness of my teacher Miss Reynolds.
The happy laugh of my best friend.
The great love of my mum.

I will put in the box . . .
A world with peace and loving hearts.
The joy of my family.
The first word I spoke.

I will put in the box . . .
The cleanest, bluest sky.
The friendship God gave me.
The colour of the yellow beach in the hot sun.

I will put in the box . . .
A colourful and peaceful flower bed.
The calm sea that just sways back and forth.
The coldest Christmas.

My box is made from shining gold, marble and wood.
I shall bury my box under the coldest snow
On the highest mountain ever.

Taylor Nicholson (10)
St Peter's RC Primary School, Cardiff

The Magic Box
(Based on 'Magic Box' by Kit Wright)

I will put in the box . . .
My very first unique teddy bear,
The brightest day in history
And the first sight of my baby brother Christopher.

I will put in my box . . .
My favourite wish that I have made,
The wonderful future of the world
And the key to the lost door of happiness.

I will put in the box . . .
The reddest sky on an autumn morn,
An ancient charm bracelet of my great nanny's,
Even answers to all the questions.

My box is fashioned from the softest silk,
Coolest marble, scented petals on the side,
Hinges of tentacles, rainbows in the corners
And the scales of a crocodile on the lid.

I shall place my box on a cloud,
And let it float in a
Great big, beautiful, bright, blue sky.

Jessica Caitlin Sidney (9)
St Peter's RC Primary School, Cardiff

The Magic Box
(Based on 'Magic Box' by Kit Wright)

I will put in my box . . .
The winning goal for my favourite team,
The signature of my favourite player
And the best goal ever scored.

I will put in my box . . .
The first laugh of my baby sister,
The smell of a freshly cooked dinner,
And the coldest winter when I am tucked up warm in bed.

I will put in my box . . .
The memories I treasure most,
The finest people I've ever met,
And the days I most enjoy with my sisters.

My box is made from the smoothest marble,
The most shiny and sparkly diamonds ever,
And the most expensive rubies that ever existed.

I shall hide my box away even from my best friends,
So they can't find it and know all my secrets,
Because my box is the most special thing to me.

Shane Geoghegan (9)
St Peter's RC Primary School, Cardiff

One Question From A Knife

I want to give up being a knife
I've been a knife too long

I want to be an innocent tin
Held in the hand of a trustworthy child
And to be put down on a hard, shiny surface
And to be opened very carefully

I want to give up being a knife
I've been a knife too long

I want to be a hair clip
Fastened into place by a gentle mother's hand
And to be worn all day by a peaceful child

I want to give up being a knife
I've been a knife too long

I want to be a soft cushion
To comfort an old lady when she sits down

The question is
Can I give up killing?

Ellen Lewis (9)
St Peter's RC Primary School, Cardiff

One Question From A Bomb

I want to give up being a *bomb*
I've been a *bomb* too long.

I want to be a frisky football
Playing with lovely children
And being kicked into the goal
Of a World Cup match.

I want to give up being a *bomb*
I've been a *bomb* too long.

I want to be a shimmering diamond
Around a rich man's neck
Or just an ordinary rock
Lying on the beach
Waiting for someone to climb all over me.

I want to give up being a *bomb*
I've been a *bomb* too long

*The question is
Can I stop destroying people's lives?*

Joseph Elford (10)
St Peter's RC Primary School, Cardiff

If My Dog Could Talk

I wonder if my dog could talk
If he would say he wanted a walk
Or a bone to chew,
A cat to chase?

I wonder if my dog could talk
If we would chat
About this and that?

I wonder if my dog could talk
What would he say?
A friendly 'hi!'
Or a sad 'goodbye'?

Milo Cashin (8)
St Peter's RC Primary School, Cardiff

One Question From A Fibre Wire

I want to give up being a fibre wire
I've been a fibre wire too long

I want to be a calculator
In the hand of any innocent person
And be used to help people with their maths
Whenever they are stuck

I want to give up being a fibre wire
I've been a fibre wire too long

I want to be a flower to blossom
For everyone to see how pretty I am
Or some ordinary chair
To rest someone's legs when they are tired

I want to give up being a fibre wire
I've been a fibre wire too long

The question is
Can you give up being harmful to a person?

Samantha Downey (9)
St Peter's RC Primary School, Cardiff

Tumble In The Jungle

I went to the jungle,
But nobody knows,
A big, fat monkey,
Tickled my toes.

I went by the elephant,
Blowing his nose,
I flew through the air,
Right off my toes.

I went to the giraffe,
On tippy-toes,
But couldn't even reach,
The end of his nose.

Siobhan Quigley (9)
St Peter's RC Primary School, Cardiff

The Magic Box
(Based on 'Magic Box' by Kit Wright)

I will put in the box . . .
All of my memories of Mother's and Father's Days,
The first time I saw my baby sister,
How scary I looked on Hallowe'en!

I will put in the box . . .
The first time I was a bridesmaid,
The first friends I had,
The very first time I hugged my cousin.

I will put in the box . . .
The first time I went to my friend's house,
The first time I saw a baby sucking its thumb,
The first time I saw the moon and stars.

I will put in the box . . .
All of the happy memories I've had,
The first time I went trick or treating,
The first time I played with my friends.

My box is made from gold with glittery silver spots
Which will glow in the dark and lead me to light.
I shall close my box and put it in a waterfall,
The clearest, bluest waterfall that ever existed
So fish can share my secrets.

Lauren Copeland (10)
St Peter's RC Primary School, Cardiff

One Question From A Bomb

I want to give up being a bomb
I've been a bomb too long.

I want to be an unharmed rock in a river
And be on my own.
I want to be a delicious, chewy sweet
On the sharp teeth of a child.

I want to give up being a bomb
I've been a bomb too long.

I want to be a super speed trainer
And get praise from a child.
I want to be kind and reliable
And not harm anyone or a group of people.
I want to be a wooden toy
In the safe hands of Santa Claus.
I want to be a football
Being kicked into a football net
In the World Cup.

I want to give up being a bomb
I've been a bomb too long.

The question is
Will I ever change?

Toby Andrews (10)
St Peter's RC Primary School, Cardiff

My Magic Box!
(Based on 'Magic Box' by Kit Wright)

I will put in my box . . .
The last soft petal that falls from a magnificent flower,
The freshest and most cleanest water you could ever drink,
A pair of colourful eyes from one of my beautiful friends.

I will put in my box . . .
The first glittering star that shines in a new year,
The most delicious smell of a cake baking,
The most creamy, dark chocolate in the world.

I will put in my box . . .
A beautiful blue rose from a lovely queen's garden,
An enormous, pink, dancing polar bear,
The swish of a galloping, green, fearless horse.

I will put in my box . . .
The last song of a famous prehistoric singer,
The pinkest, most perfumed, proud rose
You have ever seen in your life,
The step of a baby.

My box is made from glittering gold and sparkling silver,
Its hinges are made from perfect purple petals,
Its sides are coloured pearls in every colour,
Its lid is made from pure white snow in the shape of flowers.
I shall put my box on a mountain
Under the sea
And there it will stay forever.

Giorgia Racis (9)
St Peter's RC Primary School, Cardiff

The Magic Box
(Based on 'Magic Box' by Kit Wright)

I will put in my box . . .
    The first twinkle of a shining star,
    The piercing growl of a stripy tiger,
    The shimmer of the calmest sea.

I will put in my box . . .
    The first trickle of a tear,
    The scent of a sweet-smelling rose,
    The sparkle of a candle.

I will put in my box . . .
    The fur of a fierce animal,
    A decorated shell that glimmers,
    A drop of eternal friendship.

I will put in my box . . .
    Holy bread and wine,
    Creative admiration of the divine Bible,
    The love of my family.

My box is made from
    Diamonds and the soft petal of a flower,
    Created with stars and moon,
    Made out of golden soil mixed with golden sand.

I shall
    Bury it in an ancient oak tree's hollow,
    Where my perfect magic box is hidden away forever.

Dhana Davis (10)
St Peter's RC Primary School, Cardiff

Emotion Is . . .

Anger is red like someone is in a mood.
It sounds like a lion that has lost its cubs.
It smells like something that has gone off.
It feels like a strong piece of rock.
It tastes like a rotten lemon.

Happiness is yellow like a daffodil.
It sounds like someone had a party.
It smells sweet like a garden of flowers.
It feels like a soft towel.
It tastes like a sour sweet.

Laughter is blue like the sky.
It sounds like a bird singing in a tree.
It smells like flowers.
It feels like it is my birthday.
It tastes like a juicy apple.

Mary Shaw (10)
St Peter's RC Primary School, Cardiff

One Question From A Dagger

I want to give up being a dagger,
I've been a dagger too long.

I want to be an innocent football
Being kicked around by a young child.

I want to give up being a dagger,
I've been a dagger too long.

I want to be a noisy CD player motivating people.
I want to be a strong-blowing fan cooling people down.

I want to give up being a dagger,
I've been a dagger too long.

The question is
Can you give up being a killing machine?

Jake Andrews (10)
St Peter's RC Primary School, Cardiff

Red

Red is a Valentine's heart,
Which we get on the 14th of February.
Red is for the sunset,
Which goes at night.
Red is my Man U shirt,
Which I wear to wicked matches.
Red is blood,
That dribbles when I am cut.
Red is a rose,
That I get for my mum on Mother's Day.
Red is a bottle of wine,
That Mum will not let me drink.
Red is a show-off,
No doubt about it,
But can you imagine
Living without it?

Kaitlin Patterson (8)
St Peter's RC Primary School, Cardiff

The Storm

See lightning is striking,
The forest is cracking,
The rain will come hailing,
A flood will be rising anon,
The heavens are howling,
The thunder is bombing,
The loud winds are screeching,
The storm has come suddenly on!
But now the sky clears,
The bright sun appears,
Now nobody fears,
But soon every cloud will be gone.

Ben Elias (7)
St Peter's RC Primary School, Cardiff

Black

Black is oil,
That can make cars go.
Black is Batman,
Who can fly away and save people.
Black is a spider,
That spins webs and frightens everyone.
Black is night,
So dark and frightening when you go to bed.
Black is a spell hound,
That leads you to nowhere.
Black is a register,
That marks up all your names.
Black is cool
There's no doubt about it
Can you imagine
Living without it?

Jack Lynham (8)
St Peter's RC Primary School, Cardiff

Hunger

Hunger is brown like a mouth-watering bar of chocolate.
It sounds like something crunchy inside your mouth.
Hunger tastes like something you could eat every day.
It looks different and comes in lots of shapes and sizes.
Hunger smells breathtaking and makes you feel happy.
Hunger reminds me of something you could eat every day
Like a bag of chips or a bar of chocolate
Because they are my favourite foods.

Rachel Edwards (9)
St Peter's RC Primary School, Cardiff

Emotion Is . . .

Anger is . . .
Anger is red like a devil.
Anger is loud like a roaring lion.
Anger is sweaty like a person in a stuffy gym.
Anger is an outrageously fierce dragon.
Anger is spicy like boiling chilli.
Anger is like a furious teacher.

Happiness is . . .
Happiness is colourful like a sparkling rainbow.
Happiness is peaceful like the sweet sound of children.
Happiness is sweet like a bunch of tropical flowers.
Happiness is cheerful like a special award.
Happiness tastes like freshly baked pancakes.
Happiness reminds me of a powerful choir
Singing on a summer's day.

Laughter is . . .
Laughter is yellow like a summery buttercup.
Laughter is like happy people having fun.
Laughter is like freshly baked cakes.
Laughter is like a beautiful holiday in the sun.
Laughter tastes like juicy lollipops.
Laughter reminds me of a day out at the beach!

Sophie Manley (9)
St Peter's RC Primary School, Cardiff

Yellow

Yellow is the sun
Which brightens up the sky
Yellow is chips
Which are scrumptious to eat
Yellow is a lemon
Which squirts you all the time
Yellow is bananas
Which monkeys eat day and night
Yellow is daffodils
To celebrate St David's Day
Yellow is The Simpsons
Who commit a lot of crime
Yellow is cheese
That you can use to catch mice
Yellow is a spell hound's eyes
Which shine like the stars
Yellow is potatoes
Which are dumb and heavy
Yellow is a funny person
No doubt about it -
But can you imagine living without it?

Conor Meehan (8)
St Peter's RC Primary School, Cardiff

Red

Red is a scarlet shirt
Shining in the sunset
Red is a Wales shirt
Wales are proud of it
Red is a Man United shirt
Firing up the table
Red is Spiderman
Who saves you if you're in danger
Red is a London bus
Driving from street to street
Red is an England football fan
Darting throughout England
Red is a Wales rugby ball
Shooting through the posts
Red is a Welsh dragon
Firing through his mouth
Red is a star
No doubt about it
You could not imagine
Living without it.

Ben Parker (8)
St Peter's RC Primary School, Cardiff

Black

Black is Batman
Robin's best friend.
Black is a teacher's chair
To see the children's super work.
Black is the night
When children sleep tight.
Black is a bin bag
Where you put your rubbish.
Black is scary spiders
They will make you scared.
Black is coal
That makes steam.
Black is Coca-Cola
That fizzes down my throat.
Black is a guitar case
When you go to play guitar.
Black is a thief
No doubt about it
But can you imagine living without it?

Joseph Clarke (8)
St Peter's RC Primary School, Cardiff

Yellow

Yellow is the sun
It blazes on us all.
Yellow is 'The Simpsons'
As Bart gets in trouble.
Yellow is the curry
It burns your mouth.
Yellow is the lemon
That sweetens up your mouth.
Yellow is the banana
It's full of goodness and fibre.
Yellow are the chips
As the oil drips off.
Yellow is my merit card
For all the good things I do.

No doubt about it
But can you imagine
Living without it?

Jake Vella (9)
St Peter's RC Primary School, Cardiff

Black

Black is a bat
Which flies high up in the night sky.
Black is a spell hound
Which leads you across the world.
Black is the night
Which all the stars twinkle in.
Black is a bin
Which you stick your crisp packets and rubbish in.
Black is a bad mood
When I get angry and horrible.
Black is coal
Which you use to burn your fire with.
Black is a register
So Sir knows who's in and who's not.
Black is leather
So we can wear it on ourselves.
No doubt about it
Black is Saruman
But can you imagine living without it?

Kieran Nolan (8)
St Peter's RC Primary School, Cardiff

Blue

Blue is a sapphire,
Shining in the night.
Blue is the ocean,
Swishing in the wind.
Blue is the sky,
Which is a huge umbrella.
Blue is ink,
That makes a pen work.
Blue is jeans,
That make you look cool.
Blue is Cardiff City Football Club,
Strong and tough.
Blue is water,
Splashing in the bath.
Blue is a ruler,
Underlining words in science.
Blue is Cardiff Blues,
Who are rough and scary.
Blue is cool,
No doubt about it -
But can you imagine
Living without it?

Christian Nunan (9)
St Peter's RC Primary School, Cardiff

One Question From A Chainsaw

I want to stop being a chainsaw
I've been a chainsaw way too long

I wish that I could be a free ant
Running from danger and being able to crawl into food
And being around millions and millions of other ants.

I want to stop being a chainsaw
I've been a chainsaw way too long

I wish I could be a wallet
Passing person to person
Protecting precious things inside
And I get to be kind instead of killing people

I want to stop being a chainsaw
I've been a chainsaw way too long

The question is
Can I be an innocent thing
Instead of being a killer?

Connor Greet (9)
St Peter's RC Primary School, Cardiff

Emotion Is . . .

Anger is red like an exploding volcano
It sounds like a naughty devil
It smells mean and fierce like a lion
It feels terrible like champions being beaten
It tastes crispy like burnt toast
Anger reminds me of sadness and makes me feel creepy

Happiness is yellow like a bright sun
It sounds like laughter, like children playing
It smells sugary like cakes
It feels joyful like the Olympics
It tastes sweet like sweets and lollipops
Happiness reminds me of singing in lots of choirs

Laughter is golden like the beautiful sunrise
It sounds happy like meows from a cat
It smells beautiful like lovely flowers
It feels happy like a baby kitten being born
It tastes sweet like candy
Laughter reminds me of being on the beach.

Philippa O'Sullivan (10)
St Peter's RC Primary School, Cardiff

Emotion Is . . .

Anger is red like a volcano.
It sounds like an angry lion roaring.
It smells of smoke like a fire.
It feels boiling like the sun.
It tastes of burnt toast.
Anger reminds me of fighting with my sister.

Happiness is yellow like a daffodil.
It sounds cheerful like children playing.
It smells fresh like freshly baked bread.
It feels amazing like being a champion.
It tastes sweet like lollipops.
Happiness reminds me of the whole family
Sitting together having a Sunday lunch.

Laughter is gold like you've found some in a mine.
It sounds joyful like you've just had some excellent news.
It smells like big, orange sunflowers.
It feels excellent like you've won a gold medal.

Christy Ring (10)
St Peter's RC Primary School, Cardiff

Emotion Is . . .

Anger is red like a tomato.
It sounds like a scary cat.
It smells like a damaged car.
It feels like a sorrowful child.
It tastes like a hard rock.
Anger reminds me of fighting with my brother.

Happiness is pink like a flower.
It sounds like Heaven has opened.
It smells like plants have grown.
It feels like a soft and cuddly bed.
It tastes like a strawberry milkshake.
Happiness reminds me of when I had a friend.

Silence is white like a quiet person.
It sounds like a quiet person.
It smells like nothing in the air.
It feels like bread, plain bread.
It tastes like a sour fruit.
Silence reminds me of when everyone was quiet in church.

Sneha Babu (9)
St Peter's RC Primary School, Cardiff

Emotion Is . . .

Anger is red like a tomato.
It sounds scary like a monster.
It smells horrible like a garbage truck.
It feels like a sour strawberry.
It tastes bitter like a sour lemon.
Anger reminds me of me and my sister fighting.

Happiness is pink like a fluff ball.
It sounds joyful like people laughing.
It smells beautiful like bluebells dancing in the wind.
It feels like a soft teddy bear.
It tastes sweet like strawberries.
Happiness reminds me of music playing.

Darkness is black like a dark and damp night.
It sounds like rustling leaves through the trees.
It smells like an eaten-away apple.
It feels like cold air running across your neck
Making your hair stand on end.
It tastes like there is no flavour.
Darkness reminds me of being all alone in the dark.

Dominique Davies (9)
St Peter's RC Primary School, Cardiff

Emotion Is . . .

Anger is red like a volcano.
It sounds fierce like a tiger.
It smells burning like a fire.
It feels strong like someone pulling a rope.
It tastes hot like a chilli pepper.
Anger reminds me of a hot volcano.

Laughter is orange like a group of bright sunflowers.
It sounds joyful like children playing on the beach.
It smells sweet like a daisy.
It feels lively like a group of choirs singing.
It tastes bubbly like champagne.
Laughter reminds me of little children
Making sandcastles on the beach.

Silence is white like nothing.
It sounds silent like someone in darkness.
It smells like an out-of-date milk carton.
It feels cold and dry like inside an old, musty cottage.
It tastes sour like a strong lemon.
Silence reminds me of someone
Walking under a dark, foggy bridge alone at night.

Rachel Morgan (10)
St Peter's RC Primary School, Cardiff

Emotion Is . . .

Anger is red like a volcano erupting
It sounds like a heavy wind gushing through the window
It smells like the stench of dead bodies
It feels like the bite of a big dog
It tastes like an out-of-date carton of milk
Anger reminds me of a teacher going ballistic.

Happiness is white like an angel
It sounds like people singing joyfully
It smells like a bottle of perfume
It feels like a soft, smooth cushion
It tastes like a juicy orange.

Darkness is black like the blackout in the Blitz
It sounds like owls hooting and wolves howling
It smells like fresh air but also dustbins
It feels like a light wind brushing your hands
It tastes like fear in the hearts of brave men
Darkness reminds me of going to bed in the dark
When I was young.

Philip Campigli (10)
St Peter's RC Primary School, Cardiff

Emotion Is . . .

Anger
Anger is red like blood
    It sounds like a car engine roar
    It smells like a rubbish tip
    It feels like a cold, hard piece of metal
    It tastes like hard and stale bread

Laughter
Laughter is green like grass
    It sounds like someone playing in the park
    It smells like fresh daffodils in the breeze
    It feels good to laugh
    It tastes like cakes in my mouth.

Darkness
Darkness is black like a broken light
    It sounds like a *roar!*
    It smells like a wet dog
    It feels like everyone is against you
    It tastes like mud that has been stood on!

Connor Price (10)
St Peter's RC Primary School, Cardiff

What Is Pink?

What is pink?
A sunset is pink,
So pretty in the sky.
What is red?
A tomato is red,
Babies can be fed.
What is blue?
A river is blue,
Shining under the sky.
What is white?
Some paper is white,
Where someone can write.
What is yellow?
Winnie the Pooh is yellow,
That can be a cuddly bear.
What is green?
A fern is green,
That can shine.
What is violet?
A crayon is violet,
That you can colour with.
What is orange?
A goldfish is orange,
That always shines like treasure.

Madi Parle-Smith (7)
St Peter's RC Primary School, Cardiff

What Is Pink?

What is pink?
A pig is pink
On a farm with other animals.
What is red?
A red rose is red
In your back garden.
What is blue?
Water is blue
In a stream when it's bubbling.
What is white?
Snow is white
When it's snowing in the cold winter.
What is yellow?
A daffodil is yellow
When you go into your garden.
What is green?
A frog is green
In a pond with lily pads.
What is violet?
A purse is violet
In your bag.
What is orange?
A tiger is orange
In the wild with other wild, crazy animals.

Chelsea Beaumont (8)
St Peter's RC Primary School, Cardiff

Emotion Is . . .

Anger is red like a bowl of blood
It sounds mad like death
It smells like a rotten strawberry
It feels scary like a monster
It tastes like a rotten egg
Anger reminds me of a wrestling match.

Happiness is yellow like a shining sun
It sounds like music playing
It smells like freshly cut grass
It feels like you are at a football match
It tastes like a slice of pizza
Happiness reminds me of children playing.

Laughter is green like grass
It sounds like children playing
It smells like chicken curry
It feels like soggy chips
It tastes like you have swallowed a fly
Laughter reminds me of Mr Moruzzi telling a joke.

Ryan Donovan (9)
St Peter's RC Primary School, Cardiff

Emotion Is . . .

Anger is red like devils' eyes.
Anger is loud like bustling cars.
Anger is sweating like a person in a big gym.
Anger is outrageously fearless like a big dragon.
Anger is sour like a sherbet sweet sizzling in your mouth.
Anger reminds me of a charging, angry teacher!

Happiness is yellow like the sizzling sun in summer.
Happiness is loud like children playing outside.
Happiness is sweet like tropical flowers.
Happiness is joyful like a gold medal.
Happiness is sweet like freshly baked cakes.
Happiness reminds me of a sweet choir singing.

Silence is white like an empty room.
Silence is nothing at all.
Silence is old, rotten food.
Silence is alone like a spare cage.
Silence is gone-off milk.
Silence reminds me of a soulless life.

Eleanor Davis (9)
St Peter's RC Primary School, Cardiff

Emotion Is . . .

Anger is . . .
Anger is grey like a stormy day.
Anger sounds like a volcano erupting.
Anger smells like a brick wall being demolished.
Anger feels like a time bomb exploding.
Anger tastes like rotten eggs.
Anger reminds me of a hulk.

Silence is . . .
Silence is white like nothing at all.
Silence sounds like a high-pitched scream.
Silence smells like thick smoke.
Silence feels like you are alone.
Silence tastes bitter and cold.
Silence reminds me of a sleeping life.

Darkness is . . .
Darkness is black and bleak like a dark night.
Darkness sounds like a howling wolf.
Darkness smells like moist, damp grass.
Darkness feels like you are being watched.
Darkness tastes like stale biscuits.
Darkness reminds me of a knife.

Jonathan Dart (10)
St Peter's RC Primary School, Cardiff

Emotion Is . . .

Anger
Anger is black like a car tyre
It sounds like people screaming
It smells like burnt toast
It feels horrible like Wales losing
It tastes like gone off milk
Anger reminds me of Wales' rugby team losing.

Happiness
Happiness is white like an angel's wings
It sounds like Heaven singing
It smells like sweet bread
It feels soft and furry
Happiness reminds me of Wales beating England!

Silence
Silence is grey like nothing
It sounds like a ghost
It smells like a black mist
It feels like something scaring you
It tastes like something sour
Silence reminds me of an empty playground.

Adrian Williams (9)
St Peter's RC Primary School, Cardiff

Emotion Is . . .

Darkness
Darkness is black like the sky at night.
Darkness sounds like creepy noises.
Darkness smells like a flame of fire.
Darkness feels like you're alone.
Darkness tastes like sour milk.
Darkness reminds me of when I'm alone at night.

Happiness
Happiness is yellow like the sun.
It sounds like people singing.
It smells like baked cakes.
It feels like the soft wall.
It tastes like juicy sweets.
Happiness reminds me of when something is really soft
And you lie on it and have a nice nap.

Anger
Anger is red like a volcano.
It sounds like thunder and lightning.
It smells of smoke like flames of fire.
It feels like a bumpy cobblestone road.
It tastes of sour water.
Anger reminds me of when someone shouts or falls over.

Lauren Leslie (9)
St Peter's RC Primary School, Cardiff

From A Window

From a window I can see
Clouds as light as a feather
Floating across the sky,
Autumn leaves twitching towards the ground
And the flowers ripening and spreading their petals.

From a window I can smell
Freshly cooked dough just coming out of the oven,
The grass swaying in the cool breeze
And the fresh air running through my hair.

From a window I can hear
The birds cheeping far and near,
Children playing hide-and-seek
And my friends shouting through my window, 'Come and play!'

From a window I feel
Welcomed into God's world,
I feel open and I can do anything I want.
I feel free.

Kate Ryan (10)
St Peter's RC Primary School, Cardiff

Valentine's Day

Roses are red, violets are blue
Today there is something special to do
Teddy bears and kisses all for you
We'll go to the cinema just us two
We'll watch Romeo and Juliet kissing all the way through
Because today my Valentine is you!

Megan Thomas (8)
Thornwell Primary School

America

I can see people splashing and swimming in the clear blue water.
I wish I could see all the magical shows and plays.
I love tasting all the delicious sweets and ice cream.
I can smell cakes and buns as I pass the cake shop.
I like to smell the mouth-watering burgers and hot dogs.
I like to taste jam doughnuts with cream and toppings on top.
I like to feel the hot sand sizzling in the sun.
I like to feel animals' fur brushing through my fingers.
I love to hear the water smashing on the enormous rocks.
I like to hear fireworks in the dark.

Daniel Wroe (11)
Thornwell Primary School

Things Found In The Wicked Queen's Pocket

Some old, smelly, slimy false teeth.
A ripped and a rough corset.
A magic mirror glowing in the dark wood.
A wand sparkling in the dark night.
A gross, wet apple sitting down on the damp floor.
A crown sparkling like magic.
A scary disguise hung up in the cupboard.
A bronze, clean comb twinkling in the sun.

Jacob Graham-Dobrowolny (8)
Thornwell Primary School

Things Found In Sleeping Beauty's Pocket

One shimmering, spinning, golden ring to go on a finger.
A cherry-coloured clip shimmering in the sunlight.
One shimmering, cool, gemmed crown.
One white handkerchief ready to be used.
One gold, stamped letter ready to be posted.
One spinning golden coin on a milk lid.
One beaded bracelet on a princess's hand.

Brittany Oliver (7)
Thornwell Primary School

Hate

Hate is black like a raging storm,
It reminds me of school on a Monday morn.
It smells like smoke hovering in the air all day.
It tastes like a cake that's starting to decay.
It feels like walking on coal with bare feet.
It sounds like my heart going *beat, beat, beat.*
And sometimes it looks like a huge black cloud
Drenching us all until the hate dies down.

Kelsey Gittoes (11)
Thornwell Primary School

Sadness

Sadness is blue like a river of tears.
It looks like pain in a room full of sunshine.
It reminds me of me and my friends breaking up
And not getting back together again.
It smells like some rotten sprouts.
It sounds like rocks falling off a big cliff.
It feels like I am about to cry in front of someone.
It tastes like something I have never tasted before.

Ashleigh Ann Fawcett (9)
Thornwell Primary School

Happiness

Happiness is yellow like a bright yellow sun.
It smells like flowers in the summer's breeze.
It looks like fresh green grass swaying in the wind.
It sounds like the calm ocean.
It tastes like a red juicy apple.
It feels like a soft fluffy pillow.
It reminds me of a happy family eating a picnic.

Rachael Sims (10)
Thornwell Primary School

Sadness

Sadness is blue like a lonely, running river.
It sounds like a thousand whales screeching.
It feels like your heart has a plug
And all happy memories drain away.
It reminds me of homeless people with no food.
It looks like a rainy day.
It smells like damp soil full of worms.
It tastes like sour milk gone off for weeks.

Stacey Gittoes (11)
Thornwell Primary School

Happiness

Happiness is red like the sunset in the sky
    It feels like it is in your heart
Happiness smells like the breeze in the sky
    It sounds like the song of the ice cream van
Happiness looks like people picking flowers in the summer
    It tastes like smooth Galaxy chocolate.
Happiness reminds me of people smiling all over the world.

Lucy James (11)
Thornwell Primary School

Love

Love is pink like floating hearts
It looks like a silk, pink, magic carpet
It smells like flowers blowing in the wind
It tastes like hot, milky chocolate that melts in your mouth
It reminds me of hugs and kisses
It sounds like candles flickering during a couple's first kiss
It feels like a warm hug from your grandma.

Skye Taylor (11)
Thornwell Primary School

Happiness

Happiness is light blue like the marvellous sky
And with the warm clouds.
It sounds like happy children laughing with their friends in the sun.
It looks like friends sticking up for each other
And playing together and having fun.
It feels like walking hand in hand down the beach
With the sunset out.
It reminds me of when me and Skye
Were riding down Balwalk shops on our bikes.
It tastes like a big bowl of ice cream on the table
Being ready to eat.
It smells of roses in the bright blue
And green fields in the gleaming sun.

Charlene Williams (10)
Thornwell Primary School

Anger

Anger is like an explosive volcano
Anger tastes like red-hot chilli peppers
Anger smells like a warm, explosive kettle
Anger looks like a jug of hot chilli
Anger reminds me of my brother in a bad mood
Anger sounds like a firearm when a fire is raging.

Luke Payne (10)
Thornwell Primary School

Hate

Hate is purple like balls of gas shooting through the sky.
It sounds like water crashing on rocks.
It tastes like pure sour lemons trickling down your throat.
It smells like men's aftershave spraying in my face.
It feels like teeth knocking together.

Cade Beacham (10)
Thornwell Primary School

Sadness

Sadness is dark blue like the ocean shining in the sun.
It looks like tears running down your face
When you've just had a fight.
It tastes like the deep ocean's salty water.
It smells like the flowers from a cemetery.
It sounds like a widow in a chair crying.
It feels like a bolt of lightning hitting you.
It reminds me of when I fell out with my friends.

Amy Huyton (11)
Thornwell Primary School

Anger

Anger is like a red, exploding volcano.
Anger sounds like screeching bats.
Anger tastes like a soapy throat.
Anger smells like a sour grape.
Anger reminds me of falling out with my friend.
Anger looks like an angry chimpanzee.
Anger feels like a stinging nettle.

Ryan Harley-Powell (11)
Thornwell Primary School

Love

Love is pink like blooming flowers.
Love smells like perfect perfume.
It sounds like an angel going up to Heaven.
It feels like I've walked through the gateway to Heaven.
It tastes of sweet hot tea.
It looks like a tower of hearts.
It reminds me of a beautiful angel.

Ryan Palmer (10)
Thornwell Primary School

Love

Love is pink like a flock of flamingos
With their pink feathers fluttering around.
It reminds me of when I got my dog Cammy.
It tastes like the sweet, warm taste of tea.
It smells like the best perfume in the whole wide world.
It sounds like a church piano playing at a wedding.
It looks like a rainbow of pink fluffy hearts.
It feels like lying on a comfy bed with pink fluffy heart pillows.

Marcus Arrowsmith (10)
Thornwell Primary School

Things Found In The Elf's Pocket

Some shiny leather for making posh shoes.
Some sparkling magic laces threading and going through holes.
Some sparkling shoe polish polishing posh shoes.
Some shiny sewing doing magic jumpers.
Some posh, shiny shoes doing magical stuff.
A magic needle threading through shoe holes.
Some gold money cart-wheeling round and round.
A shiny map showing special ways.

Alex Methuen (8)
Thornwell Primary School

Fear

Fear is black like the night sky.
It sounds like weird noises that you can't describe.
It feels like sickness in your stomach.
It tastes like rocks and stones.
It looks like a pitch-black room.
It reminds me of the screech of bats.
It smells like a house that has been around for a hundred years.

Robyn Evans (10)
Thornwell Primary School

Things Found In Rapunzel's Pocket

A bracelet shining like other colours.
A map sparkling like some gold.
Some glittering hair bobbles from the dressing table.
A pencil and notepad to draw a lovely apple tree.
A picture of her mum and dad in a frame.
Some lovely food.
Some money to buy some food.
Some hairspray smelling like flowers.
A lovely drink of apple juice.
A shining compass looking to the north.

Jennifer Thomas (7)
Thornwell Primary School

Untitled

One sparkling bobble that is feint.
Some shiny paper that glitters in the dark.
A red sparkling hair band that shines.
A nice shining bow on a dress.
Some shining money in a pocket.
A nice pencil that can draw.
A map showing the way to the park.
A crown that shines in the dark.

Yiesha Weir (8)
Thornwell Primary School

Things Found In A Little Pig's Pocket

A sparkling, silver coin cartwheeling down the village.
A fluffy handkerchief that tickles you.
A thin straw that makes you sneeze.
A fat paper than can fold itself.
A magic pencil that can write by itself.
Some sparkling food that when you eat it you can fly with it.
A big map the size of a car park.

Sophie Gresswell (8)
Thornwell Primary School

Manchester United

M illwall is the team that we beat in the FA Cup Final.
A lex Ferguson is the name of the manager.
N eville is one of our top players.
C oach is the person that trains our players.
H enry is one of our worst enemies at goal.
E agle's one of our reserves.
S chole is a top midfielder.
T im Howard is the name of our keeper.
E vening matches for us to play.
R ed is the colour of their kit.

U nited fans coming to watch matches
N ervous team when they play a hard side.
I rwin is one of our players that does not play as he is old.
T im Howard is not very good, he is our reserve keeper.
E xcited players if they are in the starting 11.
D jemba is the name of our reserve.

Daniel Tyler (9)
Thornwell Primary School

Helicopter Ride Over The Grand Canyon

The sight of red rocks falling over 10,932,105km
And splashing into a blue river.
I can hear our pilot's voice echoing in my ear
Giving me information.
I hate the feel of the sweltering sun burning me to death.
I like to smell the pilot's deodorant smelling of coconut.
I love the taste of peppermint gum I've chewed for an hour.
It's exciting to see the people and things in the rocks.
I wish I could hear my mum's excited scream.
I would like to feel the red precious rocks.
I can smell my sister's sweat dripping off her head.
I can still taste the sticky pink doughnut I had for breakfast.

Harriet Ling (10)
Thornwell Primary School

Under The Table

The boy sat under the table,
He didn't know what to do.
He looked around for something
And then undid his shoe.

The girl sat under the table
Eating a pot of glue.
She pulled her hair and sat on a pear
And never went to school.

Jonathan Davies-Whyatt (9)
Thornwell Primary School

Fear

Fear is black like the sky of the underworld.
It reminds me of eating sprouts.
It tastes like the salty sea of the glaciers.
It feels like getting squashed
Between two of the world's most jaggedy rocks.
It looks like the burning of Heaven and the lightning of Hell.
It smells like a rat to a ghost.
It sounds like a stampede of buffalo.

Mason Segal (11)
Thornwell Primary School

Love

Love is pink like a strawberry
It tastes like a love pie that has just been made
It smells like a perfume in the air
It looks like a field covered with flowers
It feels like soft feathers
It sounds like hands playing harps
It reminds me of when I watched 'Free Willy'.

Edward Neal (10)
Thornwell Primary School

My Best Friends!

My best friend is Kayla,
She really is a strayer,
She is a really good swimmer,
She's always been the winner!

My second best friend is Chloe,
She wishes she was called Zoë,
She's got really nice hair,
She's got her own little pink chair!

My third best friend is Jemma,
Her mum's name is Emma,
She wishes she was cool,
So she could always rule!

My final best friend is Jess,
She wishes she was the best,
She bought her own pet bunny,
That was extremely funny!

Abigail Watts (11)
Thornwell Primary School

Shark

A horrid fish is a shark
A cold-blooded killer
A fish assassin
A leg snatcher
Teeth gnasher
Jaw gangler
A horrid sight to see
The one, the only shark
Boat biter
Man hunter.

Jordan Gough (10)
Thornwell Primary School

Walking Through The Countryside

I wish to hear green wavy grass tickling my feet,
I'd love to feel the shy, tiny animals,
I would like to see the clouds gathering together
To spell my name,
I wish I could see aeroplanes flying through tunnels
Then fly into the misty clouds,
I can smell smoke coming from chimneys
In the shape of love hearts,
I'd love to taste strawberry ice cream
With a huge Flake melting into my mouth,
I wish I could see a green water swimming pool
As deep as the tallest man on Earth,
I would like to feel the fluffy clouds and get into them
And they'd take me on holiday every day,
I would like to smell a man's bakery shop so I could go there,
I'd like to hear animals telling me what's on their minds.

Tracey Roberts (11)
Thornwell Primary School

Don't Get Your Knickers In A Twist!

She's a wonderful moaner just like Homer.
She should be on Yelling Idol *not* Pop Idol.
She's shopping mad just like super mad.
She's a party animal sort of like the Queen.
She's a boy hater with a mirror to throw at.
She sings a lot like Britney Spears.
She's on a diet and she's going mad with no proper food to eat.
She's a dancing lover just like Justin Timberlake.
She's got a worldwide smile which sparkles when she moves it.
She always marches upstairs and screams and always . . .
Gets her knickers in a twist!

Kirsten Jones (11)
Thornwell Primary School

Anger

Anger is red like the glaring rays of the sun,
It smells like suffocating smoke,
It tastes like chillies cooking your insides,
It looks like a large stone mangling your body up,
It reminds me of an earthquake destroying the Earth.
It sounds like the embers of a crackling fire.
It feels like you are in a flaming inferno.

William Tregaskes (10)
Thornwell Primary School

Anger

Anger is red like hot lava running down a volcano.
It feels like a big hand pinching you.
It tastes like rotten eggs which have been in a bin for years.
It reminds me of revenge and pain.
It sounds like dinosaurs roaring.
It looks like horrible bears eating.
It smells like a ball of fire.

Ellie Neye-Williams (10)
Thornwell Primary School

Hate

Hate is dark red like blood
It tastes like chocolate, cold and dark
It looks like giant flames in a dark room
It reminds me of anger and pain
It smells like smoke and hot lava
It sounds like an explosion
It feels like a football in the face.

James Edinborough (10)
Thornwell Primary School

The Stable

I see a beautiful chestnut bay in the field called Star.
I spot a dun fowl called Coco galloping through a stream.
I love to hear whinnies of a black stallion cantering in a field.
I hear the hooves of beautiful grey pony trotting in the paddock.
I feel tack wax all over my hands.
I like to feel Star's silky muzzle in my hand.
I hate the smell of crunchy orange carrots.
I taste a huge, crunchy, juicy apple.
I taste bits of yucky golden hay.

Sophie Bennett (10)
Thornwell Primary School

My Best Friend

My friend is as nice as a teddy bear
And when I'm lonely he's always there
Out of the world he is the best
But sometimes he can be a pest
We sometimes argue, we sometimes fight
But it always turns out all right
He is like a brother to me
The greatest friend in world is Lee.

Kieran Brewer (10)
Thornwell Primary School

The Icy Winter

The snowdrops are falling as quick as a cheetah,
Freezing shivers up and down your spine,
The icy roads may make you slip,
But that's not all of it.
The breezy nights will make you freeze,
In the wintry breeze.

Lydia Ferriman (10)
Thornwell Primary School

Spooky Night-Time

There's a full moon outside,
What will I see?
Spooky shadows on the stairs,
Monsters at the window,
There's something in my sister's room,
It's starting to glow,
Shooting stars zooming past.

There's a full moon outside,
What will I hear?
Mum snoring like an ogre,
Spooky noises like
Wolves howling,
Dogs growling,
Wind whistling.

There's a full moon outside,
What do I feel?
Hairs on my back standing on end,
Sweat dripping down my face,
A cold shiver all down my body,
Something tickling my tummy,
The hand felt like a zombie's.

I wake up panting breathlessly,
I look as pale as a ghost,
It was just a nightmare,
Lucky for me!

Emma Giles (11)
Thornwell Primary School

The Monster On The Stairs

What's that up there up on the stairs?
It's horrid and hairy,
And terribly scary.
It could be the tooth fairy!
What's that up there on the stairs?

Siobhan Rogers (10)
Thornwell Primary School

My Pet Dragon

My pet dragon is fluffy head to toe
It eats anything for fun, you know
It has a lot of enemies
And friends too
It might look scary
I'm sure it's not though

My pet dragon is red
My pet dragon is big and tall
It ate my teacher
My friends and all
It just ate my parents
My bedroom as well
It's still looking hungry
It's coming this way!

Even if it's going to eat me
It's still my best friend
I'm sure it won't!
Will it?
Ooh nooooo!

Ryan Thomas (11)
Thornwell Primary School

My Cat

My cat is as fast as a cheetah
And a very fast eater
He hunts birds as sly as a tiger
And he is a very good hider
He sleeps all day especially in May
And he likes to attack hats like a rampaging rhino
His favourite place to sleep is the big, furry rug
He looks as snug as a bug on that rug.

Jack Pearce-Webb (11)
Thornwell Primary School

My Dog

My dog is a cat hunter.
My dog is a bone grinder.
My dog can run as fast as a cheetah.
My dog is so good at dodging
You can hardly see her.

My dog is a good hider.
My dogs is a fast eater.
My dog is a good ball catcher.
My dog is a good sniffer.
My dog sleeps most of the day
Especially in December.

My dog chases crows in fields.
My dog is as playful as a cat.
My dog is always on the go but
My dog is the best.

Chloe Drake (11)
Thornwell Primary School

The Furry Fish

He was called Ernie,
A lovely little fish,
He used to jump out of his bowl,
Into my dish.
Then one day he got furry,
I didn't know what to do,
So I took him in the bathroom
And flushed him down the loo.
My mum asked, 'Where is Ernie,
That lovely little fish?'
I told her the story
Now I'm swimming in a dish!

Kristie Harry (10)
Thornwell Primary School

Dog's Life

Moon-howler
Cat-killer
People-defender
Steak-eater
Street-walker
Vicious-protector
Bone-chewer
Painful-biter
Flea-scratcher
Kennel-sleeper
Loud-barker
Mess-maker
Toy-wrecker
Night-creeper
Ball-catcher.

Alex Pelling (10)
Thornwell Primary School

A Pirate's Poem

Neck-cutter
Rum-drinker
Leg-loser
Person-catcher
Patch-wearer
Gold-owner
Plank-jumper
Ship-taker
Treasure-hunter
Ship-blower
Parrot-liker.

That's a pirate's poem.

Nikaela Methuen (10)
Thornwell Primary School

My Horrible Little Sister

My horrible little sister acts like a chimpanzee
And screams as loud as the whole of England.
Here are a few words
That will tell you about my horrible little sister.

Dreadful-talker
Disgusting-eater
Dummy-sucker
Bottle-drinker
    Bad-temper
    Brilliant-shouter
    Amazing-biter
    Awful-sleeper
Attention-getter
Experienced-screamer
Excellent-slopper
Night-waker
    Nappy-wearer
    Lap-sitter
    Hair-puller
    Horrible-sister!

Lee Haines (11)
Thornwell Primary School

Fish

Bait-eating,
Smooth-moving,
Peculiar-looking,
Eye-popping,
Tank-swimming,
Water-living,
Bubble-blowing,
Scale-shining,
Fast-swimming
Fish!

Michael Lowe (10)
Thornwell Primary School

The Perfect Holiday

We went on holiday
To Portugal once.
The weather was perfect
You know.
We got on a plane,
Zoomed off to a villa
Where the lawn was perfectly
Mowed.

The villa was magnificent
And so was the pool.
Us kids stared in awe,
So much better than school.

We explored the villa,
Five bedrooms - great!
Had a little drink
And then went off shopping
As quick as a wink.

After we gazed
At the faultless view
All of the kids
Pushed my dad in the pool.

The rest of the holiday
Gone with a blur
Back to our dog
All covered with fur.

Charlotte Davies (11)
Thornwell Primary School

A Thief

A thief, a thief,
I hear him everywhere.
A thief, a thief,
Banging here and there.

A thief, a thief,
Is creeping up the stairs.
A thief, a thief,
I don't think he cares.

The phone, the phone,
Has been cut off.
The phone, the phone,
I hope he'll get lost.

The phone, the phone,
I wish it would work.
The phone, the phone,
I hope he doesn't hurt me.

I think, I think,
I hope he has gone.
I think, I think,
I think most of my house has gone!

Kyle Harry (10)
Thornwell Primary School

Winter

W arm houses today
 I ced lake. St
 N ick is coming tonight
 T rees are frozen
 E verybody rushing to
 R oaring fires to keep warm.

Shay Hill (9)
Thornwell Primary School

Angry Words

Angry words are like a huge volcano erupting fiery acid
Falling on top of people.
Angry words are like terrifying fangs
Dripping red blood down my back.
Angry words are like sharp nails
Stabbing me in my back and crushing my bones.
Angry words are like a long knife
Peeling off potato skin into a big bowl of custard.
Angry words are like huge, yellow, rotten teeth.
Angry words are like pointy horns
Digging into your flesh.
Angry words are like a spiky sword
Digging into your feet.

Chloe Adams (8)
Thornwell Primary School

The Terrible Monster

The worst monster is very mad,
And is as old as your dad.

The worst monster is never, ever clean,
But it is truly, terribly mean.

The worst monster's roar is as loud as the whole world's choir,
And its breath is as hot as a ball of fire.

The worst monster's skin is as black as the dark,
And it is as tough as bark.

The worst monster's nose is as round as a doorknob,
And its terrifying name is . . . *Bob!*

Matthew Barnes (11)
Thornwell Primary School

The Dog For Me!

There is a little dog who sits on a log
And glares with her glittery eyes.
Her nose is so black, just like a black bat
And love in her heart never dies.

All the boy dogs want her with her bright, golden fur,
So pretty and so loving (I'm not surprised!)
Her name is Milly, she is not very silly
And she's the dog in my eyes.

She's playful and cuddly, ever so snuggly
And she's the dog for me.
She guards me and wakes me to take her for a walk to run free.
Then I take her home and give her some tea.

Amie Morgan (9)
Thornwell Primary School

I Wish

I wish I could boot a ball from Africa back to France
And still score.
I wish I was a millionaire.
I wish I could beat my uncle and my dad at pool.
I wish I could fly around the world in 2 minutes.
I wish I could build an aeroplane that I could fly in the air
Far, far away and come back in 2 days.
I wish I could jump off the top of the cliff
And still stay alive.
I wish I was as good as Martin Adams at darts.
I wish I was a fantastic artist.
I wish I could dive from the top of the Chepstow church
And still stay alive.

Joel Butcher (9)
Thornwell Primary School

The Fat Black Cat

The fat black cat went under the mat to have a little nap.
The fat black cat opened the fridge to look for a snack.
The fat black cat drank some Coke and did a flip-flop.
The fat black cat did a handstand and fell on his back.
The fat black cat did a tap dance and fell into a crack.
The fat black cat went to a club, got onto the stage
And began to dance.
The fat black cat wrote a poem and it was called 'The Fat Black Cat'.

Georgia Brown (8)
Thornwell Primary School

I Wish

I wish I could have a silver jacuzzi in my bedroom.
I wish I could have a playground in the house.
I wish I could be a model when I'm older.
I wish I could be a famous singer like Anastasia.
I wish I could be the fastest person in the world
And run for England.

Shannon Smith (8)
Thornwell Primary School

Animals

A n enormous elephant trumpeting as loud as it can.
N asty tiger chasing a gazelle.
I n the jungle the cheetah is waiting to catch its prey.
M onkey swinging from tree to tree and vine to vine.
A naconda swimming swiftly in the mangrove swamp.
L ion, the king of the jungle lying in the shade.
S loth moving so slowly along the branches of the jungle.

Sam Greening (9)
Thornwell Primary School

My Dragon

Fire-spitter
Teeth-barer
Eye-glower
Evil-looker

> Tail-whipper
> Children-eater
> Long-sleeper
> Water-dreader

Booming-walker
Tongue-flicker
Village-burner
Spike-spiker

> *Scary creature!*

Holly Poole (11)
Thornwell Primary School

Excuses, Excuses!
(Based on 'Excuses, Excuses' by Gareth Owen)

'You're late again,' sighed Mr Spark.
'Yes, I got chased by a great white shark.'
'Where is your homework?'
Then the boy began to smirk,
'Aliens landed in my garden.'
The teacher's voice began to harden.
'Where's your PE kit?'
Said the teacher like a rock.
'Sorry, Sir, the reason is I lost my sock.'
'Now you can do it in bare feet.'
'That will be such a treat!'

Jasmin Davies (9)
Whitestone Primary School

Tongue Tasters

Crunchy, munchy salad that's green,
The healthiest thing I've ever seen,
Coke that's dark, brown and fizzy,
Sometimes it will make you dizzy,
Tingly, tangly sherbet sweets,
Taste delicious but wreck your teeth.
These are the things I love,
Because they are sent from up above.

Emily Stevens (10)
Whitestone Primary School

Tongue Tasters

S ometimes the potatoes sizzle on my fork,
U nlike the tender, well-cooked pork,
N ow I think I'll try some creamy mash,
D eliciously followed by gravy with a crash,
A nd now I'll have some saucy pie,
Y ou won't have a tastier lunch than I.

Kizzi Parry (9)
Whitestone Primary School

The Feather

Gracefully-swaying
Floating-flipping
Twirling-twisting
Slowly-zigzagging
Down to the ground.

Amy Smith (9)
Whitestone Primary School

Tongue Taster

Sizzling, popping pancakes,
Melting chocolate milk flakes.

Really succulent, crispy chips,
Leaves salt on your lips.

Lovely, squelchy Italian pasta,
It makes you run that much faster.

Saul Moore (10)
Whitestone Primary School

Tongue Tasters

Heavenly fruit and snow-white cream
Wake me up, it's all a dream
Tasty lollies and Dairy Milk
Slipping through my mouth like silk
Melting ice cream and strawberry jelly
Swirling, whirling in my belly.

Josie Ransome (10)
Whitestone Primary School

Tongue Tasters

I like crinkly, chompy crisps
Especially when they sting my lips
Salty, chewy chips are nice
But I prefer some refreshing cold ice
Chocolate mice are very new
But I like some refreshing stew.

Jessica Link (9)
Whitestone Primary School

The Cook

I know a funny, youthful cook,
With spotty, dotty spots,
He keeps his big, thick recipe book,
In a multicoloured box.

He has a little fluffy cat,
Who curls up by the fire,
The heat warms up her gentle nap,
As the flames rise even higher.

One day cook bought a stripy scarf,
He wore it into town,
The stripes made people laugh and laugh,
Until they all fell down!

Once cook went out in the fog,
He bumped into a sign,
He tripped over a spotty log,
And almost broke his spine.

Look at cook's menu, mmm, let's think,
There's delicious types of meats,
Coca-Cola for a drink,
Dessert is lots of sweets.

Then cook bought a pretty dress,
To deliver for a special day,
'Twas for his great old aunty Jess,
On her 90th birthday.

Katie Williams (10)
Whitestone Primary School

Excuses, Excuses
(Based on 'Excuses, Excuses' by Gareth Owen)

'Late again, Robinson.'
'Yes, Sir, I was shopping in Morrisons.'
'And why can't you do it after school?'
'Because, Sir, that is just not cool.'
'And where are your bags then?'
'I gave them to my cousin Ben.'
'Well, you're late.'
'I had to climb over the gate.'
'Now you're in detention.'
'I'd rather have suspension!'

Rhiannon Robinson (9)
Whitestone Primary School

Excuses, Excuses

'You missed the Maths test yesterday, Boris.'
'Sorry, Sir, I was in the gloomy forest.'
'The forest! Why where you there?'
'Sorry, Sir, my dog ran off without a care.'
'How fast is your speedy dog?'
'Ten times faster than that warthog.'
'Never mind, where is your homework?'
The little boy began to giggle and smirk.
'Aliens took it. Gosh! They were weird!'
And with that the boy disappeared!

Sam Davies (10)
Whitestone Primary School